AF386585

JIRI GEORG DOKOUPIL

VENETIAN BUBBLES

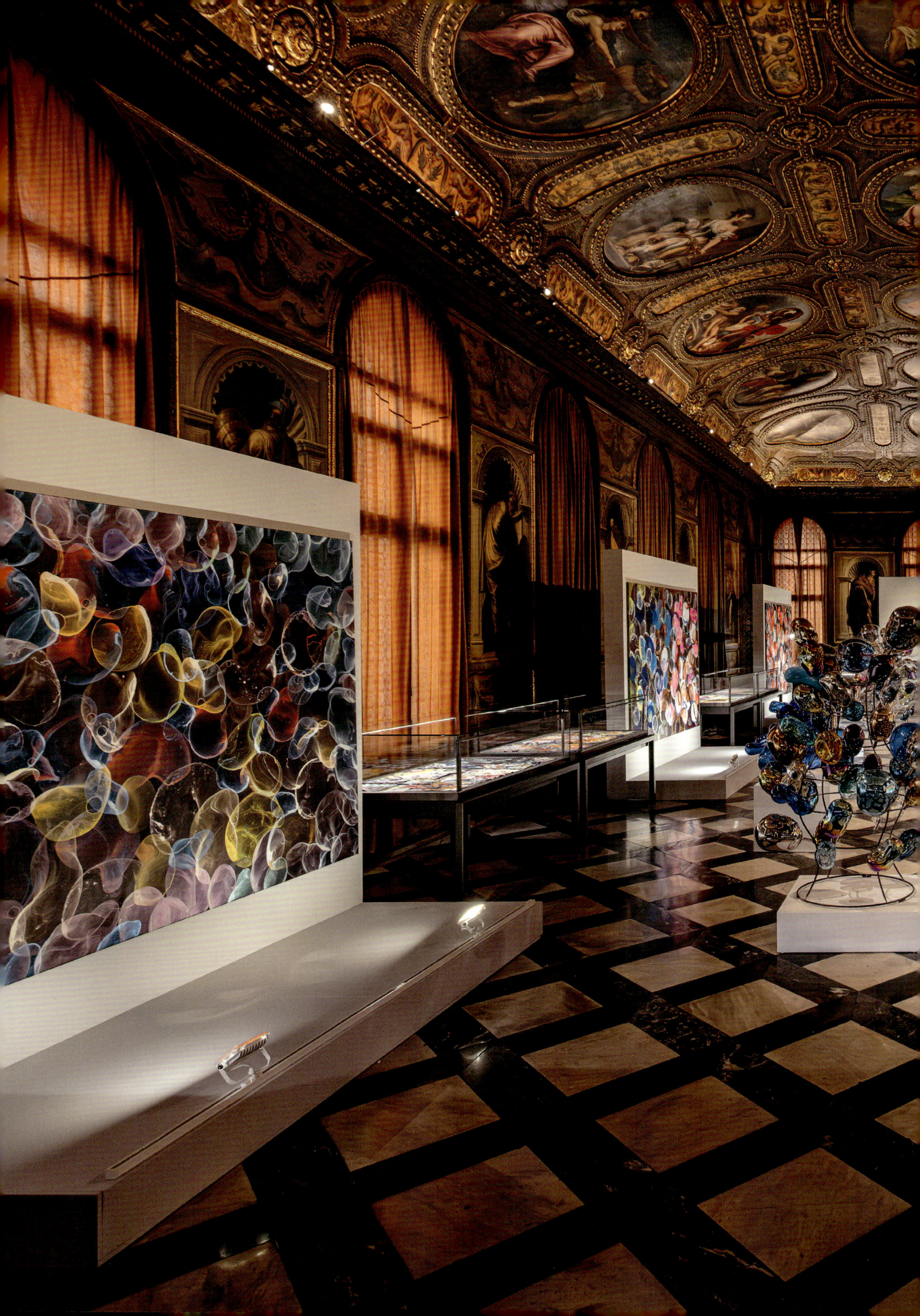

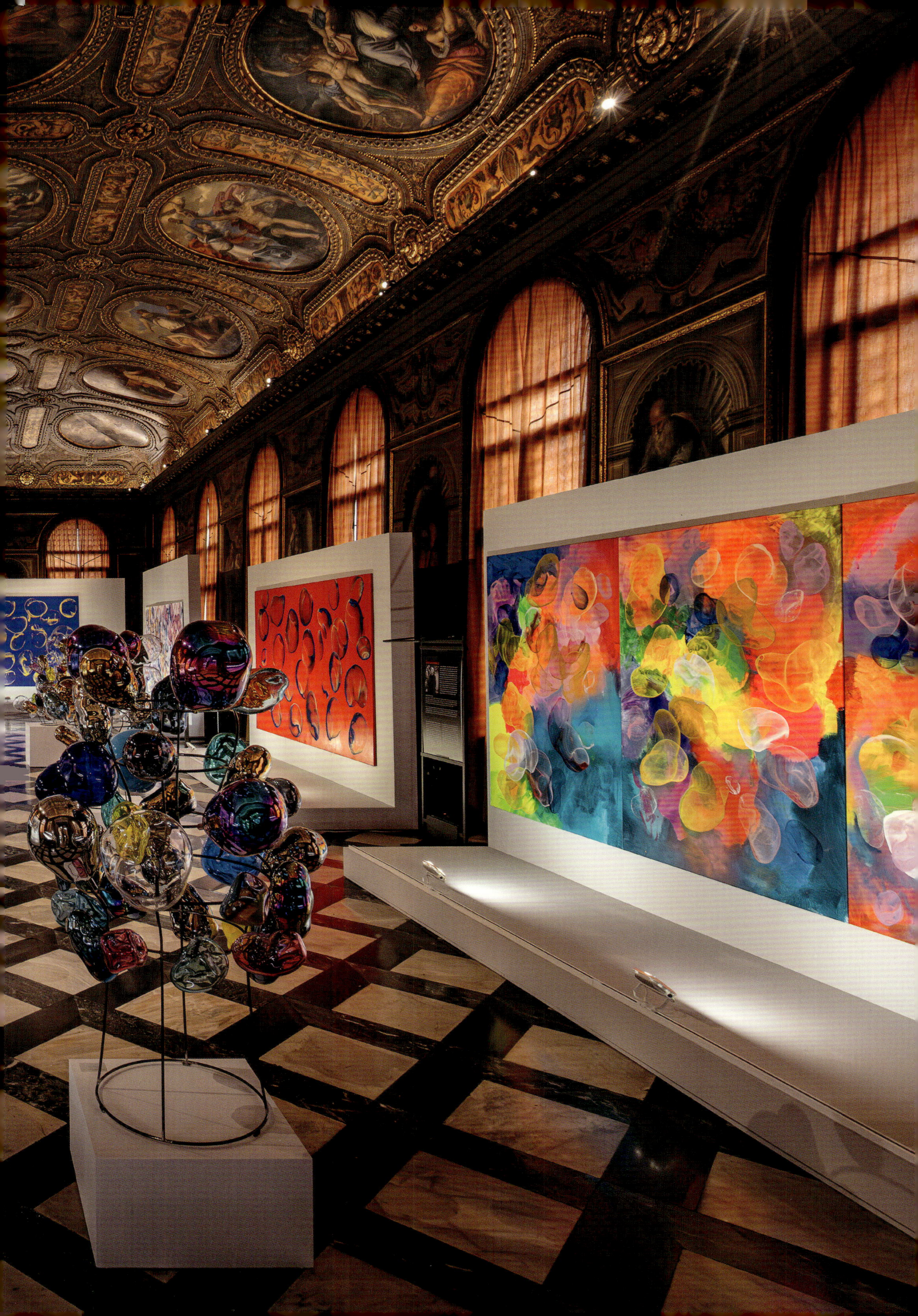

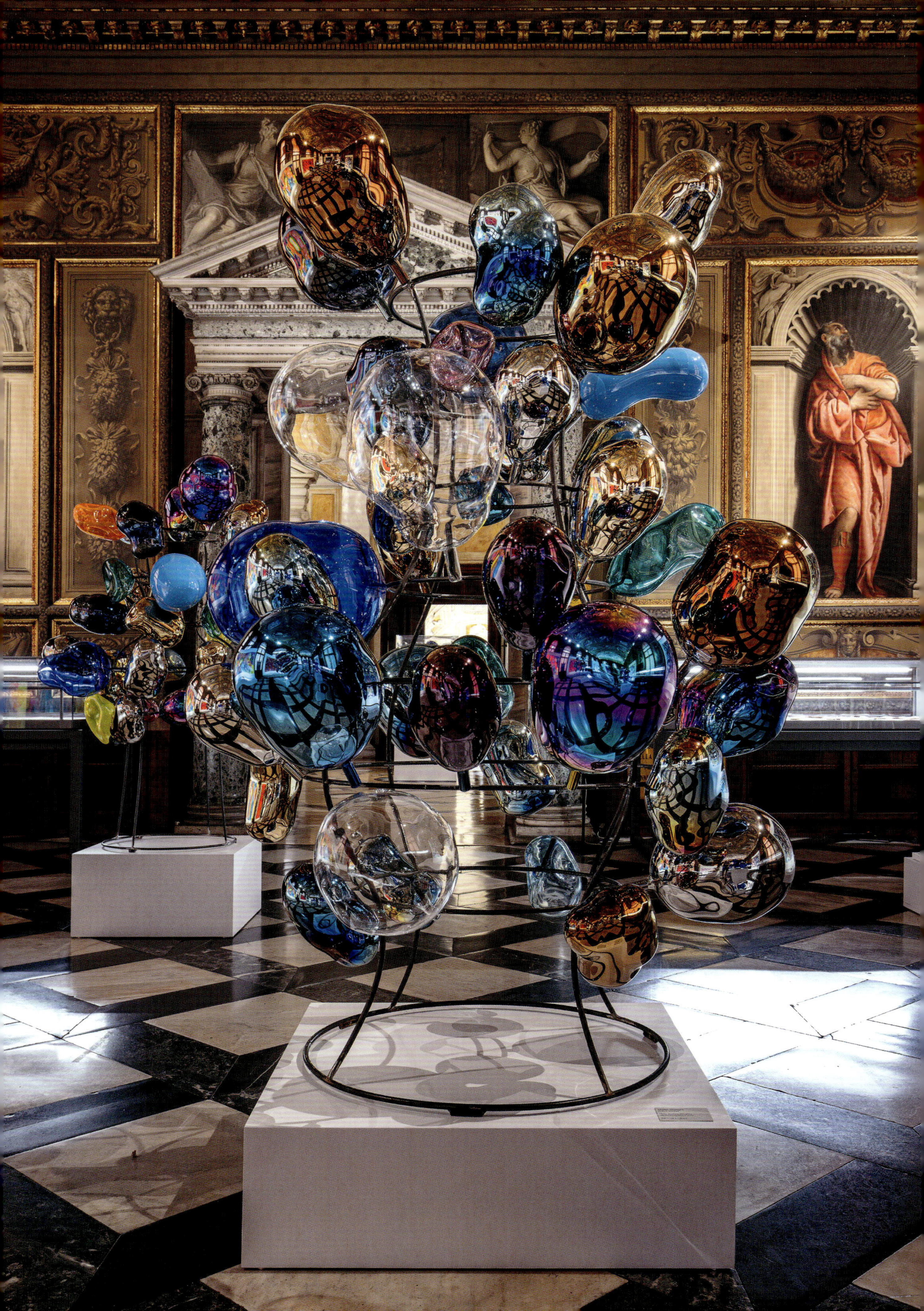

JIRI GEORG DOKOUPIL

VENETIAN BUBBLES

edited by Reiner Opoku

SKIRA

Cover
Yenni 4 (detail), 2023–24
Metal structure and glass
170 × 130 × 110 cm

Pages 2–3, 12–13, 14–15, 16–17, 18–19
Views of the exhibition *Venetian Bubbles*,
Biblioteca Nazionale Marciana,
Sale Monumentali, 2024

Page 4
Ruth 3, 2023–24
View of the exhibition *Venetian Bubbles*,
Biblioteca Nazionale Marciana,
Sale Monumentali, 2024

Page 20
Open Bubbles Condensation Cube, 2024
View of the exhibition *Venetian Bubbles*,
Biblioteca Nazionale Marciana,
Vestibolo, 2024

Page 21
Glass Assemblage I, 2024
View of the exhibition *Venetian Bubbles*,
Biblioteca Nazionale Marciana,
Vestibolo, 2024

Page 22
Ruth 4, 2023–24
View of the exhibition *Venetian Bubbles*,
Biblioteca Nazionale Marciana,
Sale Monumentali, 2024

Art Director
Luigi Fiore

Editorial Coordination
Eva Vanzella

Copy Editor
Doriana Comerlati

Layout
Antonio Carminati

First published in Italy in 2024 by
Skira editore S.p.A.
Palazzo Casati Stampa
via Torino 61
20123 Milano
Italy
www.skira.net

© 2024 The Authors for their texts
© 2024 Skira editore for this edition
© Jiri Georg Dokoupil by SIAE 2024

Printed and bound in Italy. First edition

ISBN: 978-88-572-5305-3

Distributed in USA, Canada, Central & South
America by ARTBOOK | D.A.P. 75 Broad
Street, Suite 630, New York, NY 10004, USA.
Distributed elsewhere in the world by
Thames and Hudson Ltd., 181 A High Holborn,
London WC1V 7QX, United Kingdom.

Office Reiner Opoku Project Manager
Hélène D'Aguanno

Photo Credits
All images © Studio Dokoupil, Prague
Courtesy Office Reiner Opoku
Installation Photographs: Tom Wagner

Jiri Georg Dokoupil
Venetian Bubbles

curated by Reiner Opoku

Biblioteca Nazionale Marciana, Venice
June 22 – August 18, 2024

Osthaus Museum, Hagen
November 30, 2024 – February 23, 2025

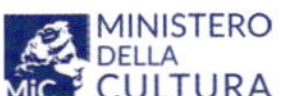

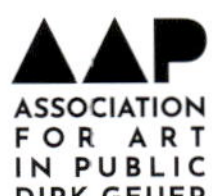

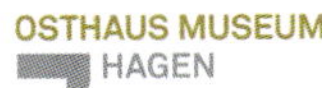

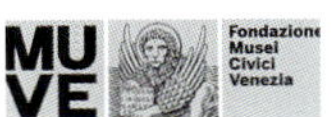

I DON'T WANT TO
BE AN ARTIST —
I WANT TO BE
A MULTICOLOURED
PARROT THAT
SPEAKS MANY
LANGUAGES.

Once again, the Biblioteca Nazionale Marciana with its own collection of Renaissance masterpieces by Titian, Veronese, and Tintoretto opens its Sale Monumentali to contemporary art, hosting from 22 June to 18 August 2024 the works of a great living artist: Jiri Georg Dokoupil.

Over the years, presenting contemporary art to the public has become a well-established habit, but what remains unaltered is above all the quality of the proposals, always of the highest standard, as is precisely the case here. Dokoupil's body of art speaks of an unconditional search for artistic freedom and maps new territory when it comes to innovative technical and experimental approaches in art. In contrast to the Old Masters' figurative artworks in the Sale Monumentali, Dokoupil's abstract bubble paintings strive to be freed of such naturalistic perfection and instead embrace randomness as the cornerstone of their composition.

The very fact that the paintings were made with real color-pigmented soap bubbles that burst on the canvas shows the innovative, creative spirit of the artist, who completely dispenses the use of a brush when applying the paint. In addition to his iconic bubble paintings, Dokoupil also transfers the theme of bubbles into the three-dimensional space for the very first time and offers the Venetian public an exclusive glimpse of his first sculptural works.

The Biblioteca Nazionale Marciana is the only institution of the Republic of Venice to have continuously operated without interruption (for a record of 556 years), maintaining its commitment to hosting contemporary art shows. It has always known how to modify and update itself over time, conserving its mission of being a place at the service of culture understood in the broadest sense. In this regard, I feel honored and compelled to continue this tradition alongside an artist as esteemed as Dokoupil. I extend my heartfelt gratitude to all parties involved in making this exhibition possible, especially to Mr. Dirk Geuer, this year's chief curator for all of Marciana's art exhibitions held in conjunction with the Biennale Arte 2024, and to Reiner Opoku for curating this show.

Special thanks go to the artist and his impressive work.

Stefano Campagnolo
Director of the Biblioteca Nazionale Centrale di Roma

I TRY TO
MAKE MY
BUBBLE PAINTINGS
MEANINGLESS

MEANINGLESS

To celebrate the awarding of the Karl Ernst Osthaus Prize to Jiri Georg Dokoupil,
in 2024–25 the Osthaus Museum is honouring the artist with a major exhibition. It gives us
great pleasure to host the very same show that was organized at the Biblioteca Nazionale
Marciana in Venice, and we are enormously grateful to our Italian colleagues for
presenting the artist's works in the lagoon city, famous the world over.
Our thanks go to everyone who has made these events possible, to all the lenders and
all the sponsors. I also wish to express my deep gratitude to Reiner Opoku, curator of
the exhibition and a friend of the artist, and to Dirk Geuer for taking the initiative to present
Dokoupil in this historic institution in St. Mark's Square. But the biggest thank-you must
of course go to the artist himself, Jiri Georg Dokoupil, without whose works the world would
be a poorer place.

Tayfun Belgin
Former Director of the Osthaus Museum, Hagen

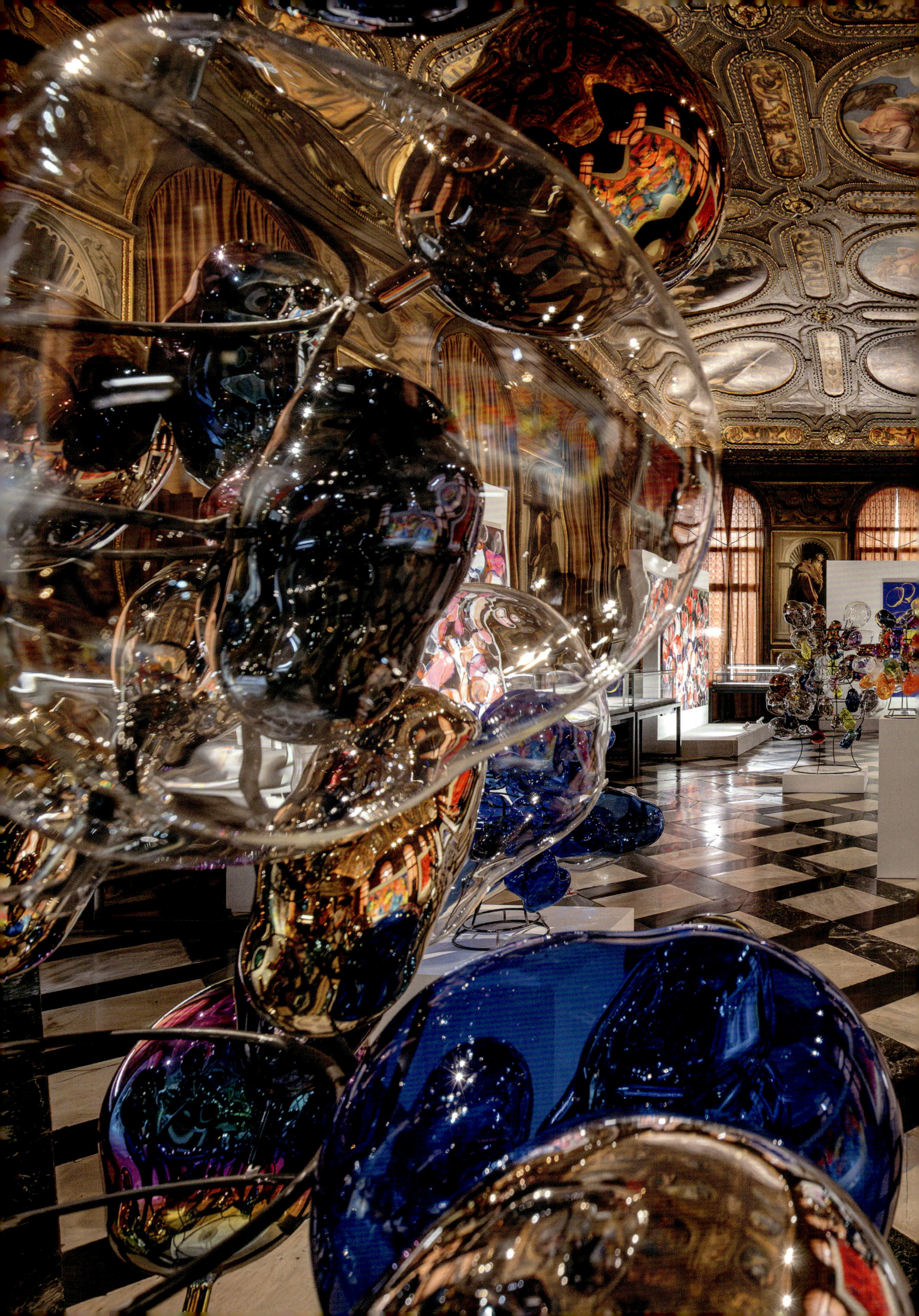

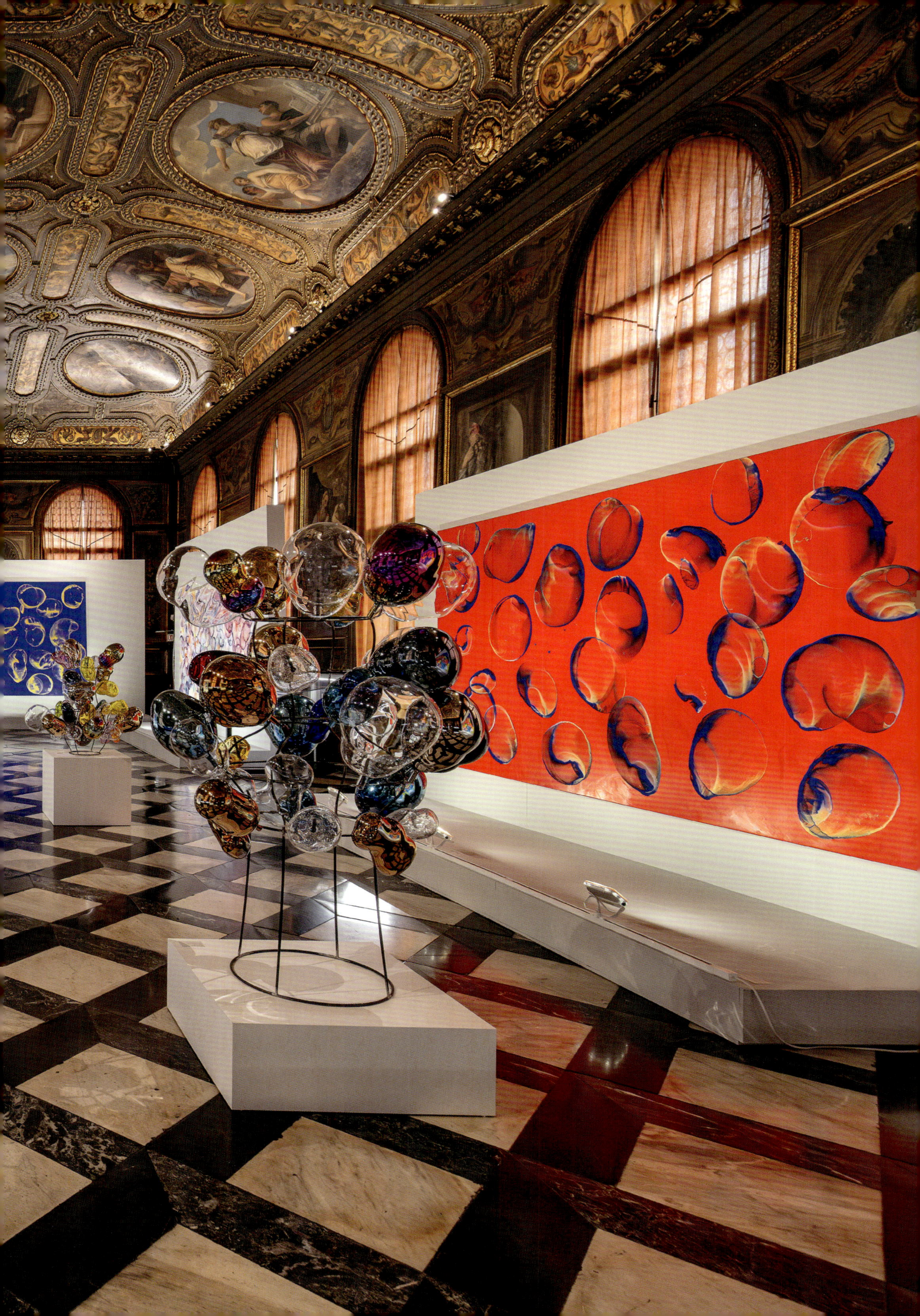

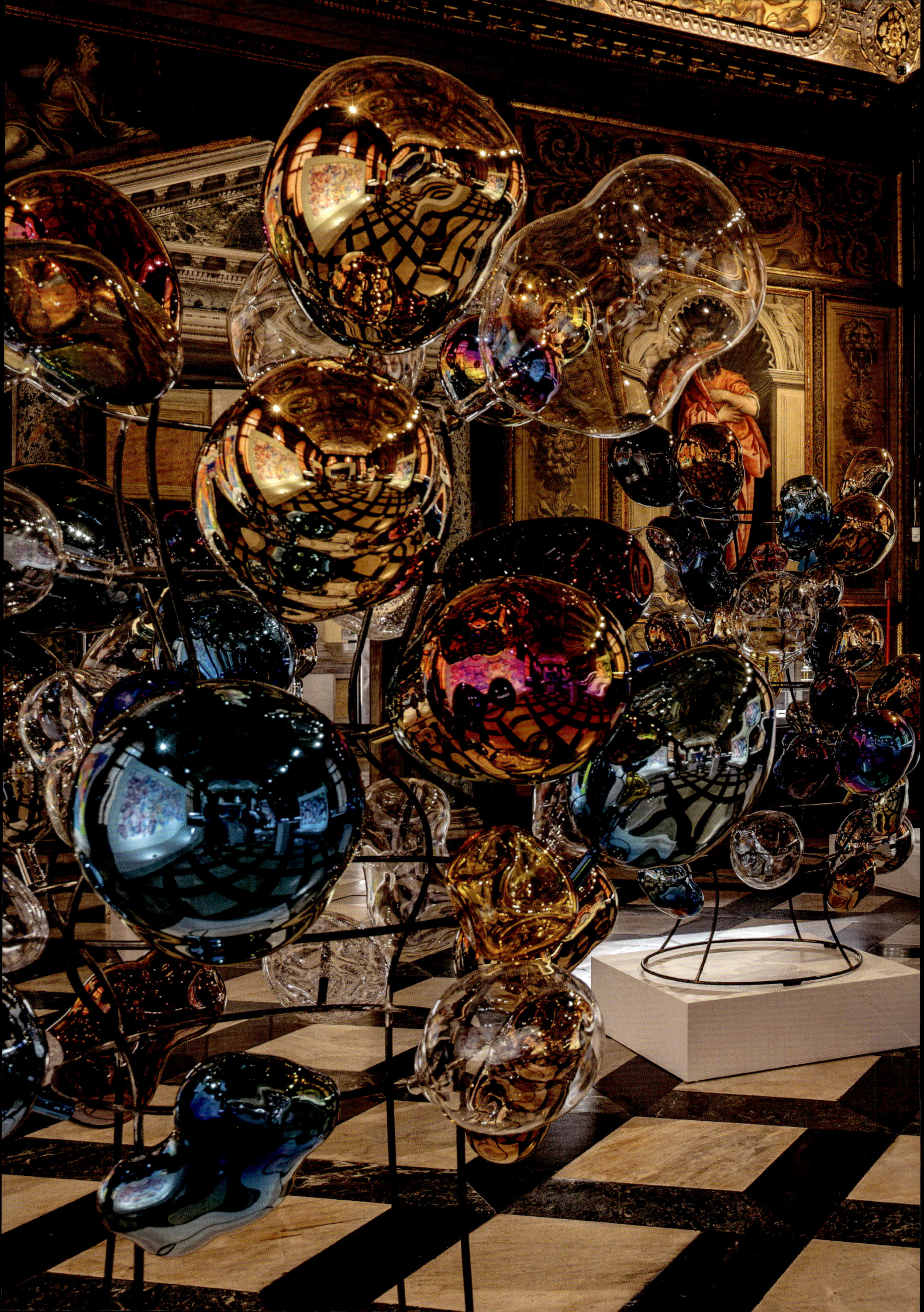

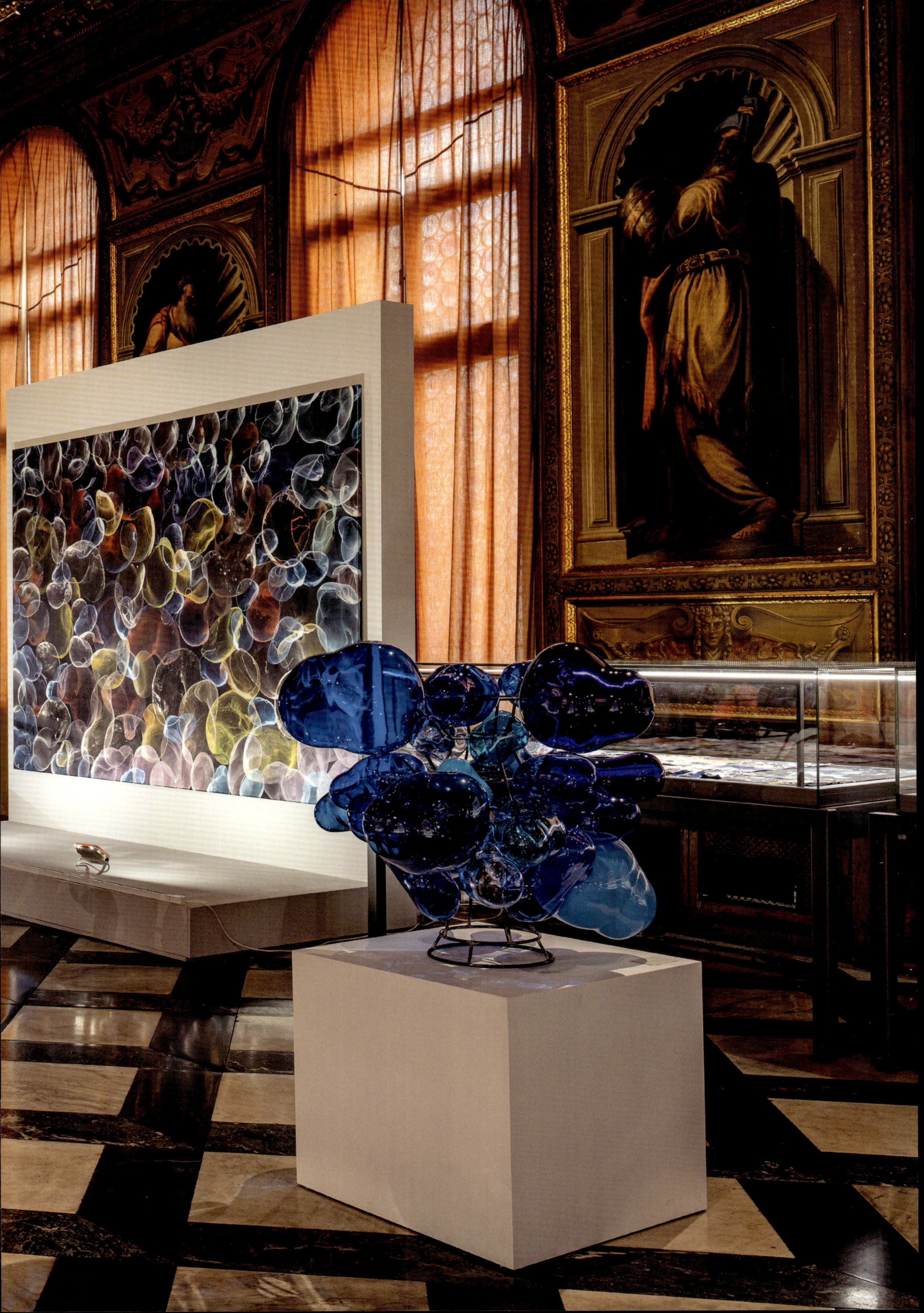

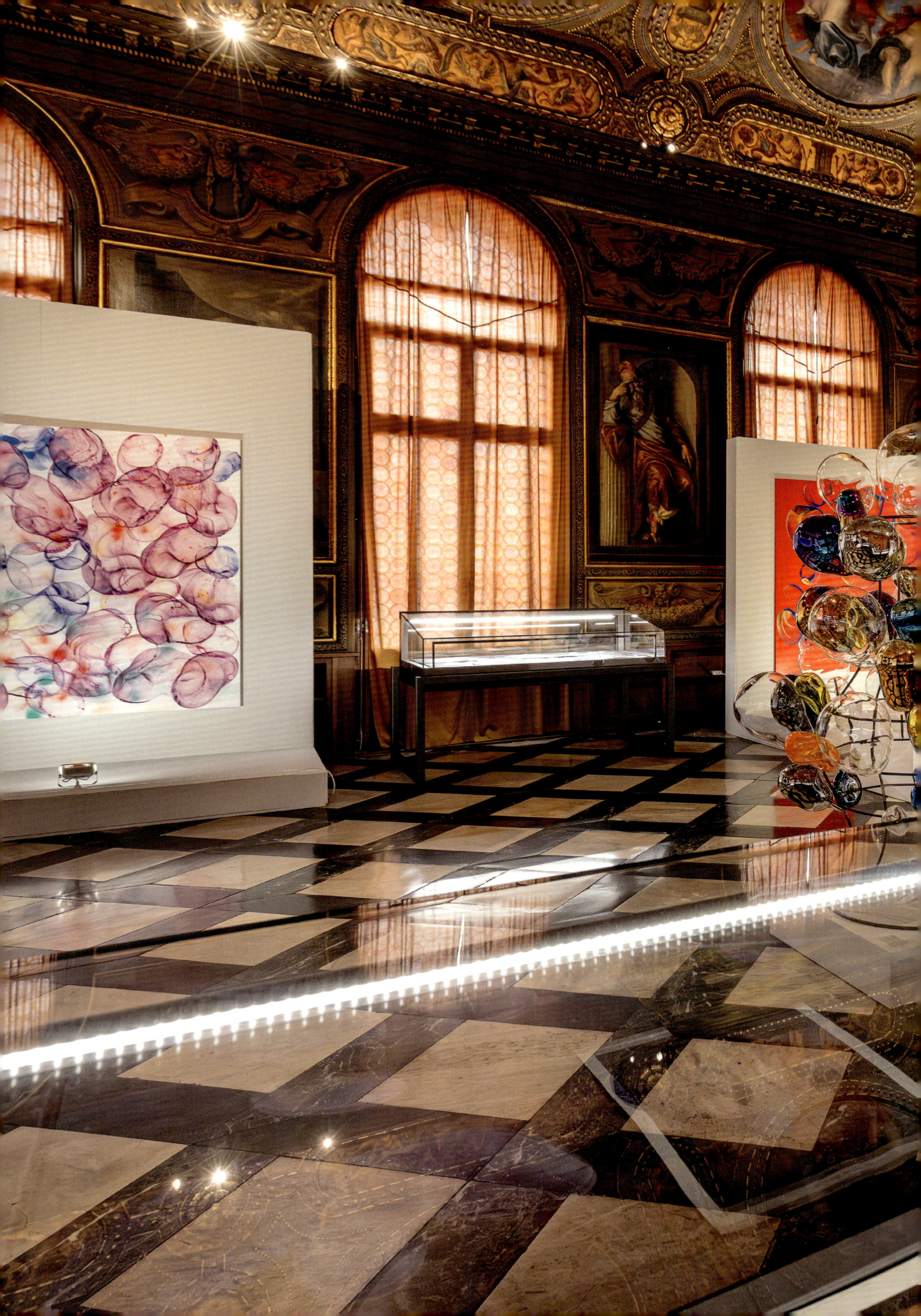

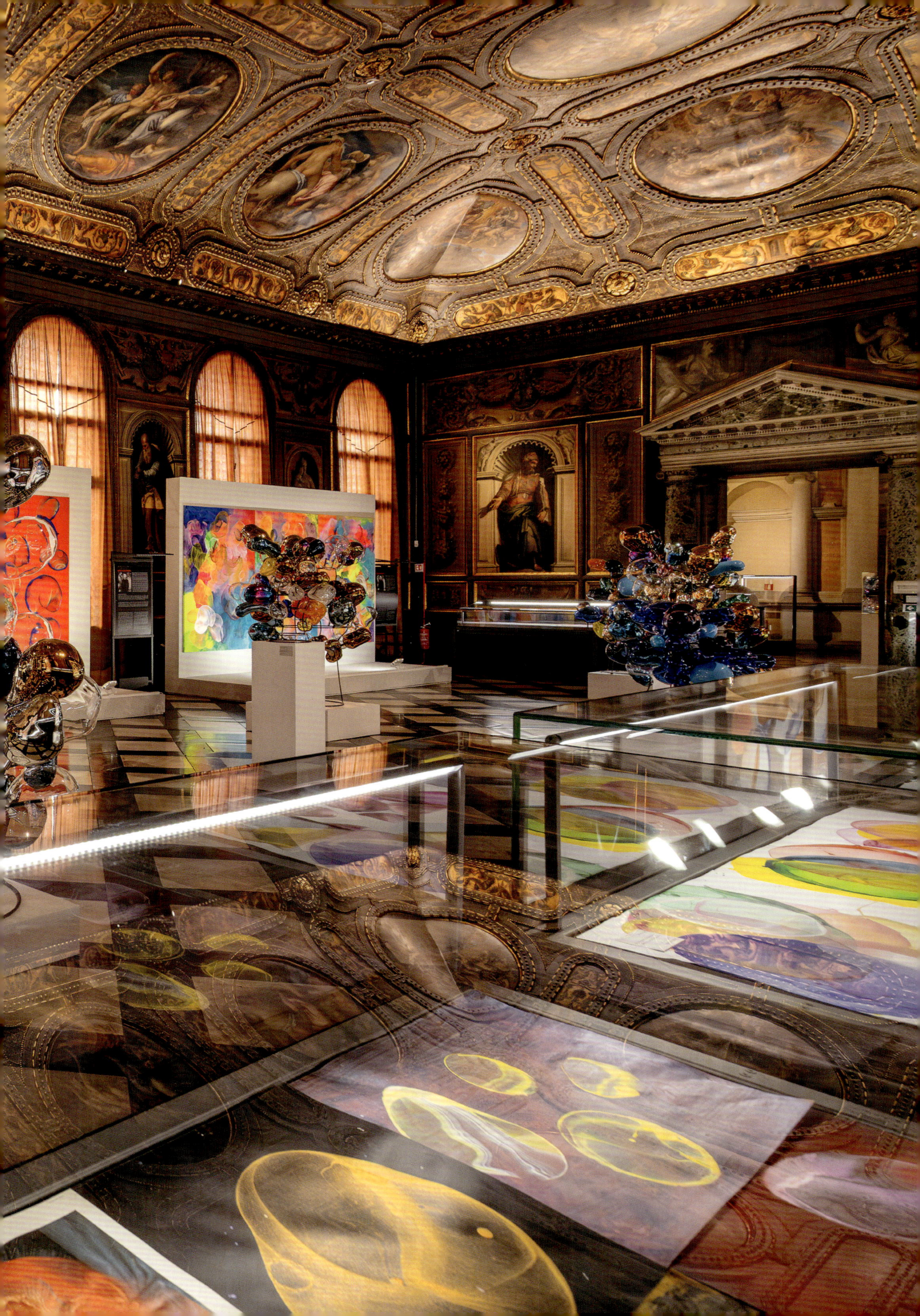

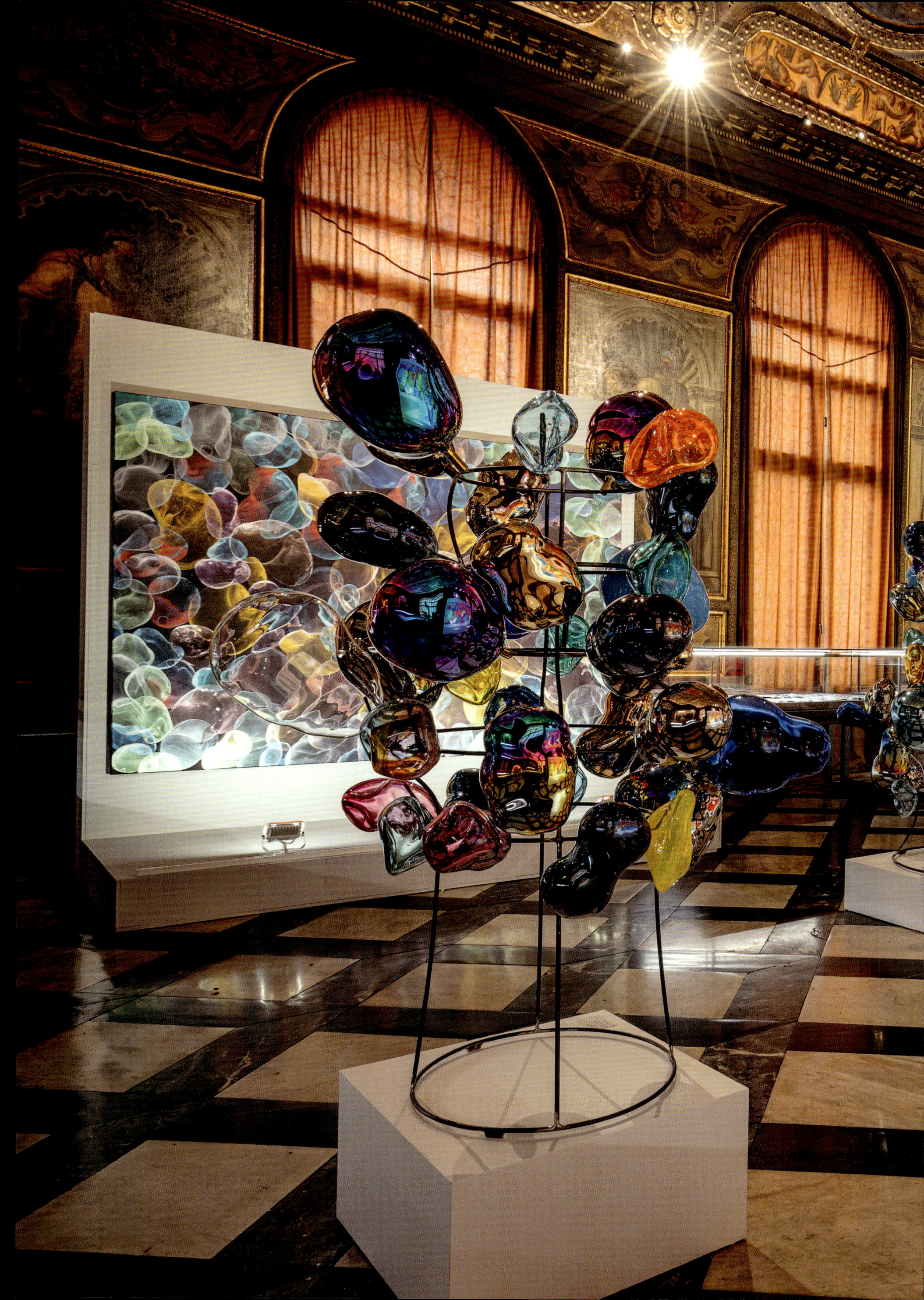

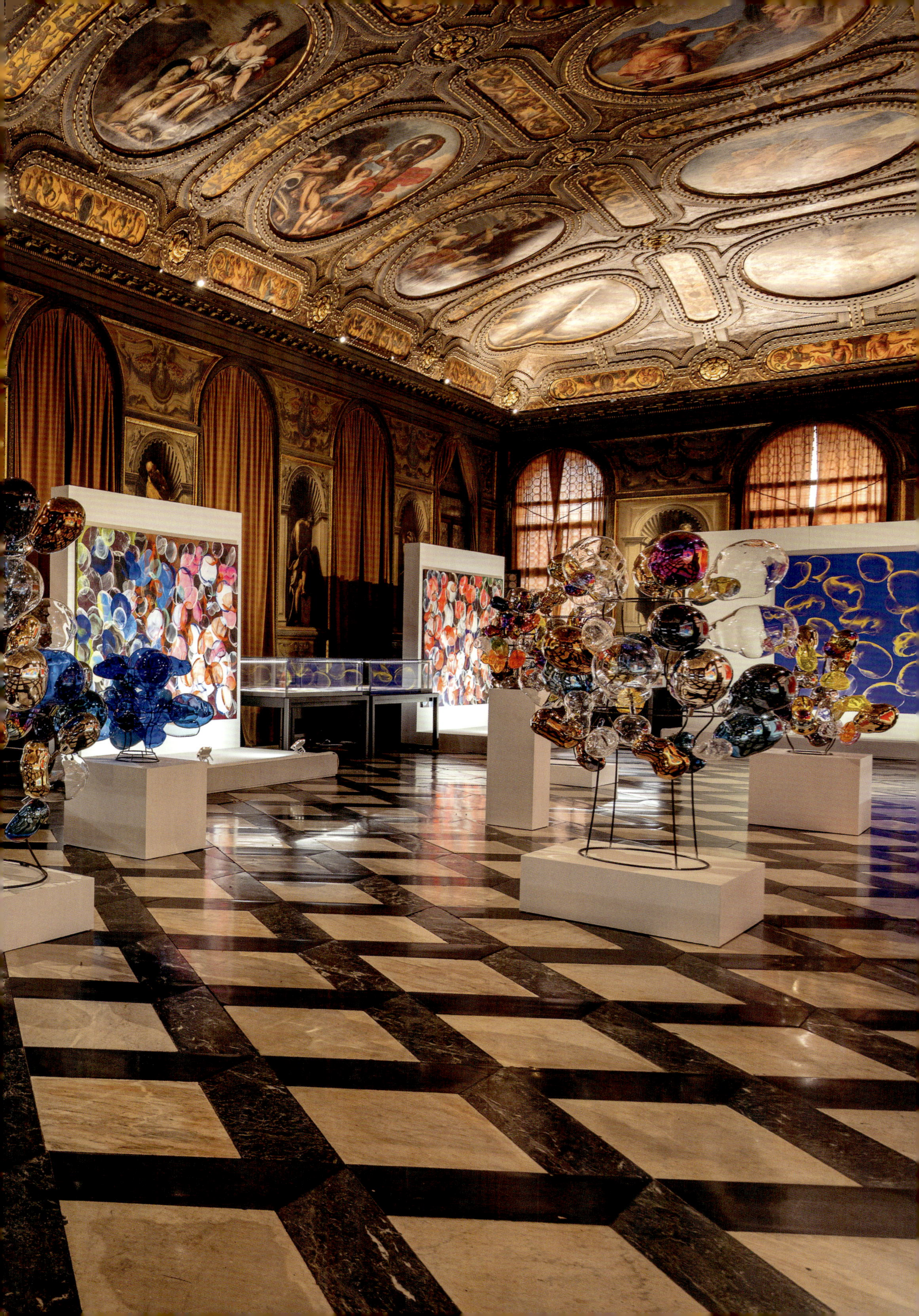

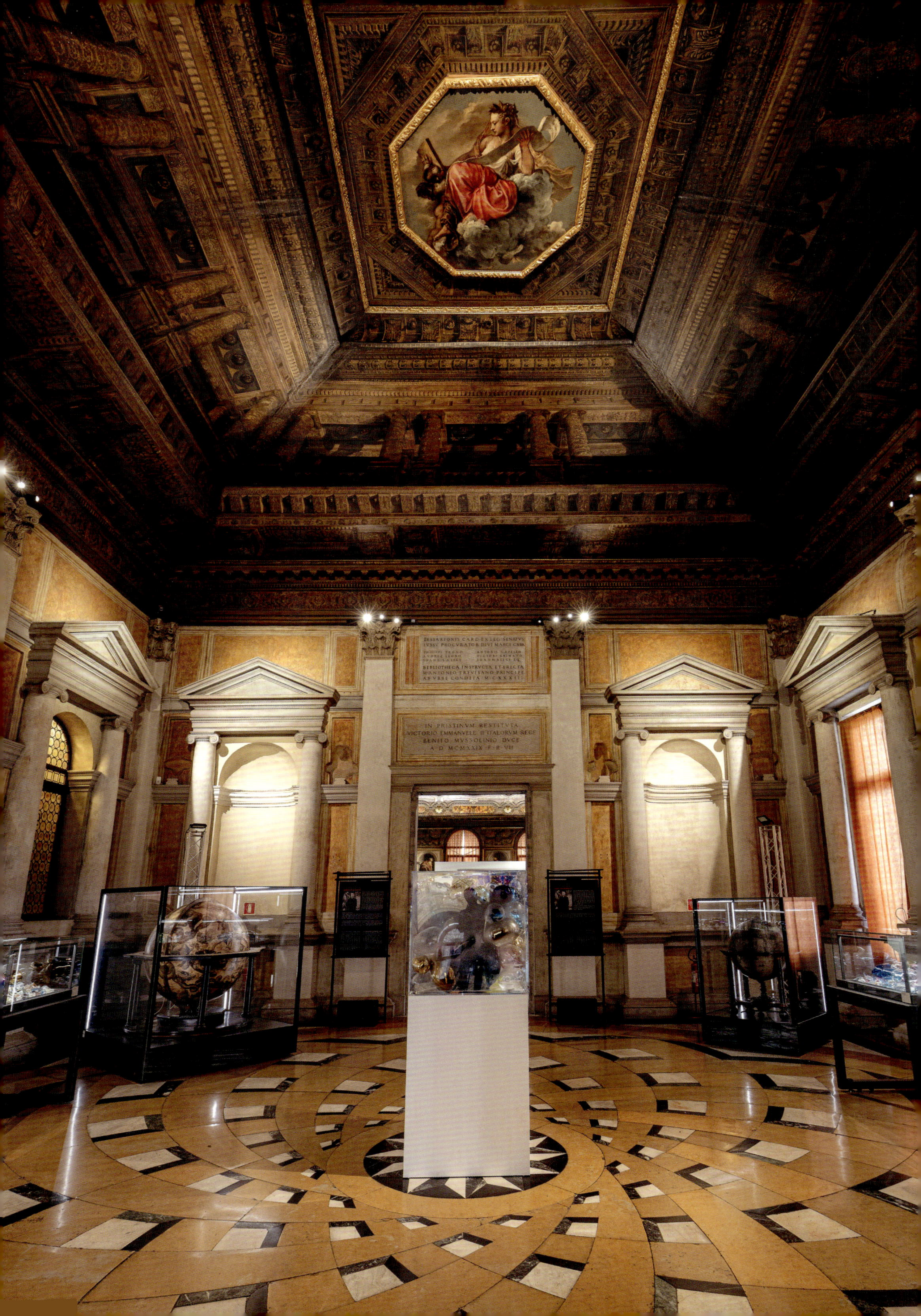

BESSARIONIS CARD EX LEG SENATVS
IVSSV PROCVRATOR DIVI MARCI CVRA
PHILIPPI TRONO ANTONII CAPELLO
ANDREE LEONE VICTORI GRIMANO
IOANNIS VALLE IOACHINI DE LA
BIBLIOTHECA INSTRVCTA ET ARICTA
M ANTONIO TRIVISANO PRINCIPE
AB VRBE CONDITA M CCXXXII
IN PRISTINVM RESTITVTA
VICTORIO EMMANVELE III ITALORVM REGE
BENITO MVSSOLINIO DVCE
A D MCMXXIX F R VII

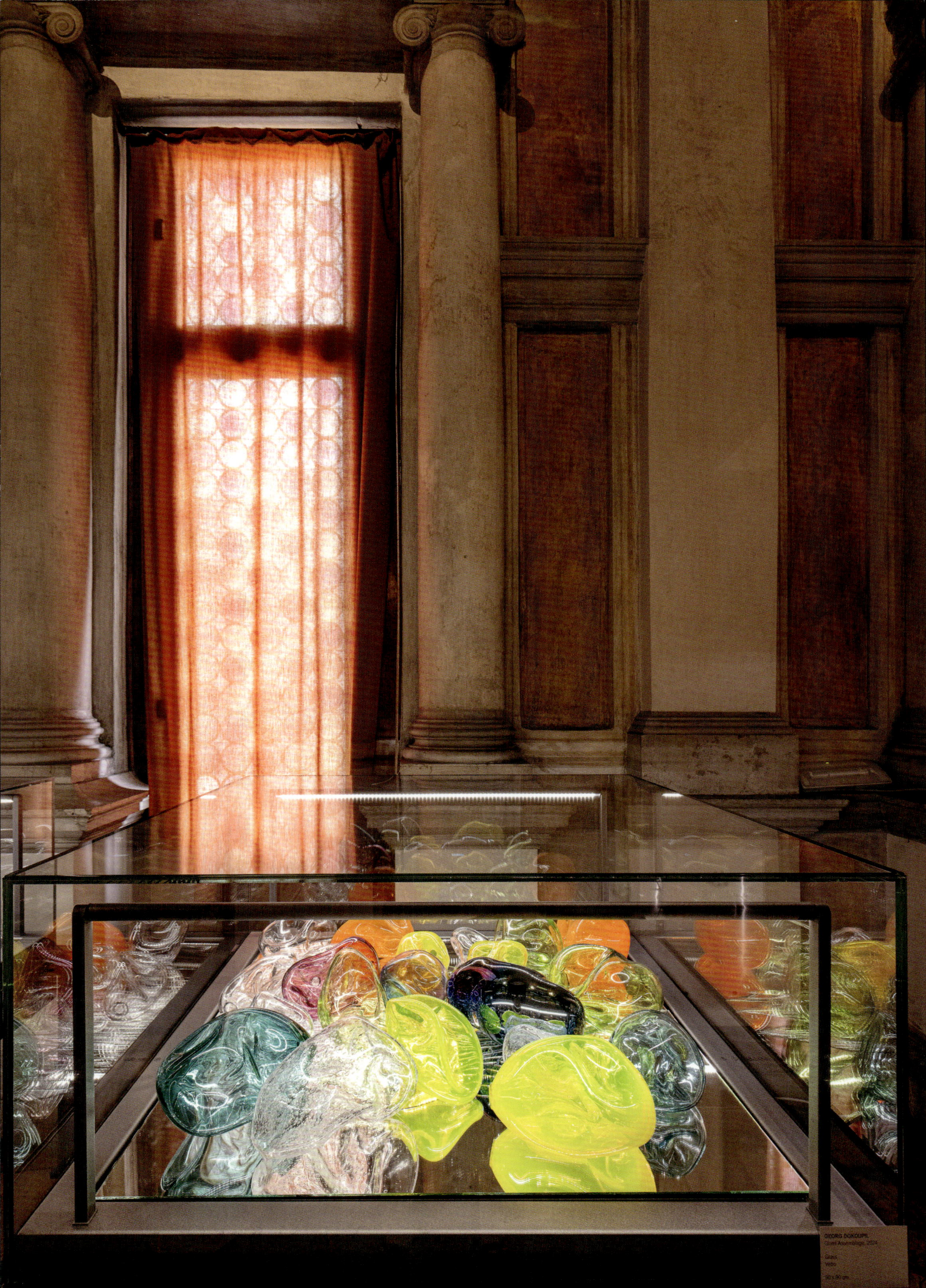

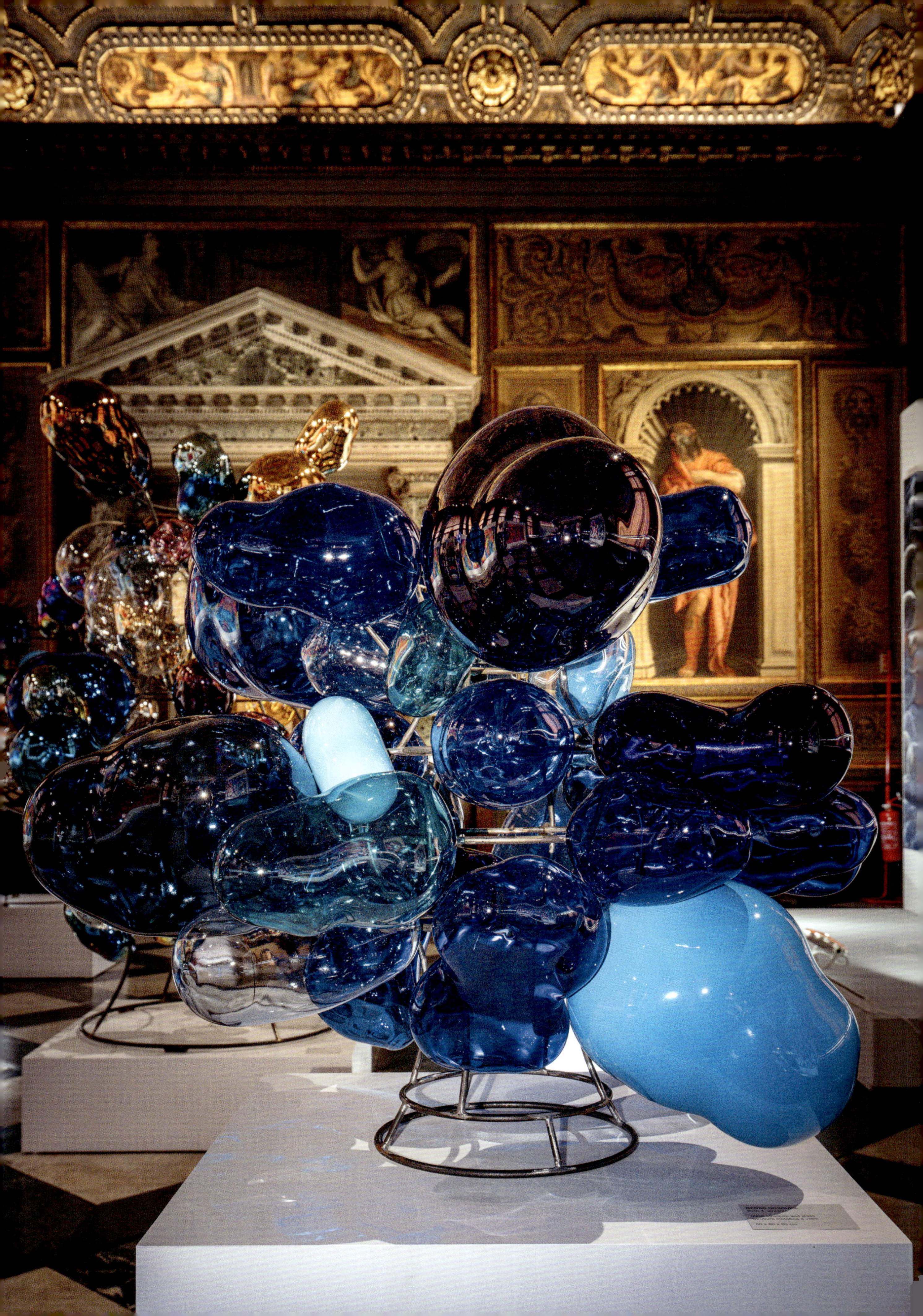

Contents

Soap Bubbles Manifesto by Jiri Georg Dokoupil
pp. 8, 10, 24, 26, 34, 35, 62, 63, 74, 75, 92, 93, 96

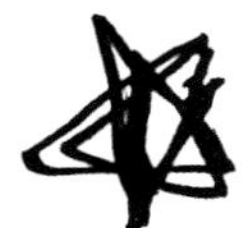

TO MAKE A
BUBBLE . PAINTING
IS ALMOST
IMPOSSIBLE AND
WHAT'S MORE
THEY DON'T
LISTEN TO YOU
AND THEY ARE
ALWAYS UPSET.

Foreword

Reiner Opoku

Jiri Georg Dokoupil is an artist overcoming genre-specific as well as physical and technical limits. Experimentation and invention have always been the driving forces in his practice. His entire career is marked by breaking with traditional painting views, switching mediums, and not committing to one style. In fact, the artist has been producing works on canvas since the end of the 1970s, and for much of that time, without the help of common painterly means. Instead, he has been using candle soot, car tires, fruit, foam, or soap to create his paintings. The freedom and the challenge of trying out anything art history has to offer and converting it into his cosmos has been a key element of his work since then.

Dokoupil's exhibition, *Venetian Bubbles*, comes once more as a surprise: Even after thirty years of working around his soap bubble painting theme, his elaborate and new group of works exhibited at the Sale Monumentali of the Biblioteca Nazionale Marciana reveals a completely new approach. He creates sculptures where his once-ephemeral soap bubbles exist as solid entities within a three-dimensional space. Cheerfully, with a dash of sassiness, he uses bottle racks to "dry" his soap bubbles, manufactured in colorful glass. The temporary character of his paintings is now in a direct dialogue with the impossible: A soap bubble captured and conserved at the peak of its existence. Fragile and shiny, colorful, and strong in its presence, Dokoupil's new sculptures radiate carefreeness and humor into the space.

In his very last sculpture – the *Open Bubbles Condensation Cube* – made as a kind of homage to his former teacher Hans Haacke, and his *Condensation Cube* from 1963–68, Dokoupil was able to create a system inside an existing system by adding glass bubbles inside a box filled with condensed water.

Through a physical process, this box evolves into an organic entity, seamlessly integrating the viewer and the surrounding environment into the artwork.

In my opinion, Dokoupil was and is a conceptual alchemist, and specifically, this very recent sculpture shows that once again very clearly.

EVERY BUBBLE—
PAINTING
IS AN EXPERIMENT.

Jiri Georg Dokoupil: Art is Not Only a Problem to be Solved but a Reality to be Experienced

Christian Domínguez

"I do not know what I may appear to the world, but to myself, I seem to have been only like a boy playing on the seashore, and diverting myself in now and then finding a smoother pebble or a prettier shell than ordinary, whilst the great ocean of truth lay all undiscovered before me." – Isaac Newton

This exhibition, *Venetian Bubbles*, curated by Reiner Opoku, invites viewers to explore the unique qualities of Jiri Georg Dokoupil's bubble paintings. Over more than thirty years, Dokoupil has used bubbles as a tool for creation, challenging conventional notions in art-making. A Czech-born artist, he emerged as a prominent figure in the international art scene during the 1980s. Born in 1954 in Krnov, Czechoslovakia (now the Czech Republic), Dokoupil later moved to Germany, initially associating himself with the Cologne art scene and the Neue Wilde (New Wild) movement.

Throughout his artistic career, Dokoupil's work has been characterized by obsessive versatility and experimentation across various mediums and styles. He gained recognition first for his dynamic and expressive paintings, incorporating diverse materials and techniques to explore themes related to consumerism, spirituality, and the human condition, reflecting the cultural and social dynamics of the time. Dokoupil's artistic practice is firmly grounded in a deep engagement with art history, combined with a playful and experimental approach to creativity. His early work often challenges established ideas about art, authorship, and the role of the artist in contemporary society. While his work has been exhibited widely in galleries and museums worldwide, it is not always understood conclusively. It remains uncertain whether Dokoupil has ever desired to be definitively understood. Perhaps the entirety of his career paths will serve as evidence that such understanding is merely a fragment of a more complex whole. In visual artistic practice, being understood is just one aspect of a multifaceted journey. In this exhibition, we will reconfirm why Dokoupil is known for his innovative approach to painting and his willingness to challenge established norms within the medium in crucial moments during his life. This long-evolving bubble paintings series can be considered as a departure from his earlier works.

With that said, let's start our journey from the side that common sense shows us as the brightest. Dokoupil's resolved self-taught position in front of painting can

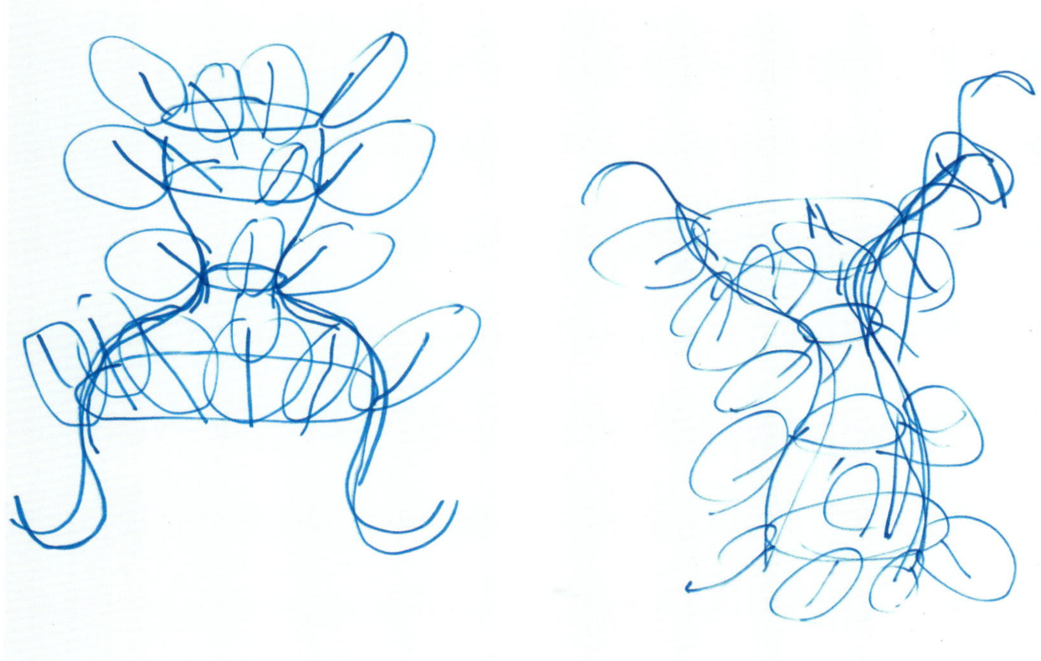

be characterized by several key aspects: a strong sense of self-determination, continuous boundary-pushing, and a powerful critical mindset. Indeed, Dokoupil actively engages with art history and contemporary discourse, incorporating these influences into his work while also subverting expectations and redefining parameters. He demonstrated a multiplicity of approaches to painting, refusing to be confined to a single style or genre, fluidly moving between them and creating a diverse body of work that defies categorization. Furthermore, his artworks possess conceptual depth, inviting viewers to contemplate deeper layers of meaning beyond the surface. Overall, Dokoupil's transition towards bubble paintings represents a complex evolution in his creative practice, driven by a combination of factors, including a desire to explore new mediums and engage in conceptual exploration. But this evolution is not simply driven by a discrete number of factors following strict logics but by a multifaceted interplay of influences, reflecting once again the organic depth and richness of his artistic vision.

This transition marks a departure from traditional painting techniques as Dokoupil embraces the inherent unpredictability of using soap bubbles as a medium. By doing so, he challenges established notions of control and permanence in art, delving into deeper themes surrounding fragility and transitoriness. Through this innovative approach, he encourages viewers to reconsider the boundaries and inner workings of painting, inviting them to engage with the ephemeral beauty of his artworks.

Now, let's provide a brief historical summary. After years of experimentation with various styles and techniques, partly influenced by conceptual teachers like Hans Haacke, Dokoupil experienced a sense of creative stagnation. Like many artists, he sought new challenges to avoid falling into repetitive patterns. Experimenting with unconventional materials and techniques reflected his desire to reconnect with more original forms of expression. This shift was motivated by a need to break free from the constraints of environmental intellectualism and ubiquitous Minimalism and Conceptualism. By diverging from his earlier influences, Dokoupil asserted his independence and rejected pressures to conform to established artistic norms. His involvement with new materials and techniques was also driven by a desire to innovate and differentiate himself from his peers, seeking to establish his originality through experimentation and risk-taking.

The evolution of Dokoupil's work since the early 1980s follows a trajectory characterized by a multitude of styles, initially inspired by Conceptualism but later diverging from its more restrictive aspects. By 1987–88, he began undertaking new directions, such as painting landscapes outdoors and creating works with whips and tires, eventually leading to the development of his candle and bubble paintings.

While the physical procedure of making the bubble paintings may seem simple at first glance – Dokoupil blows soap bubbles onto a canvas coated with paint, allowing the bubbles to burst and leave behind circular imprints – the command of materials has been a long journey for the artist. Today, Dokoupil has mastered the technique in such a way that it allows surprising and extraordinary combinations of colors and shapes. Nonetheless, if you take a closer look, you will realize that the bubble paintings are characterized by an ephemeral and organic quality. The irregular shapes and patterns created by the bursting bubbles evoke a sense of randomness and chance, highlighting the unpredictable nature of the artistic process.

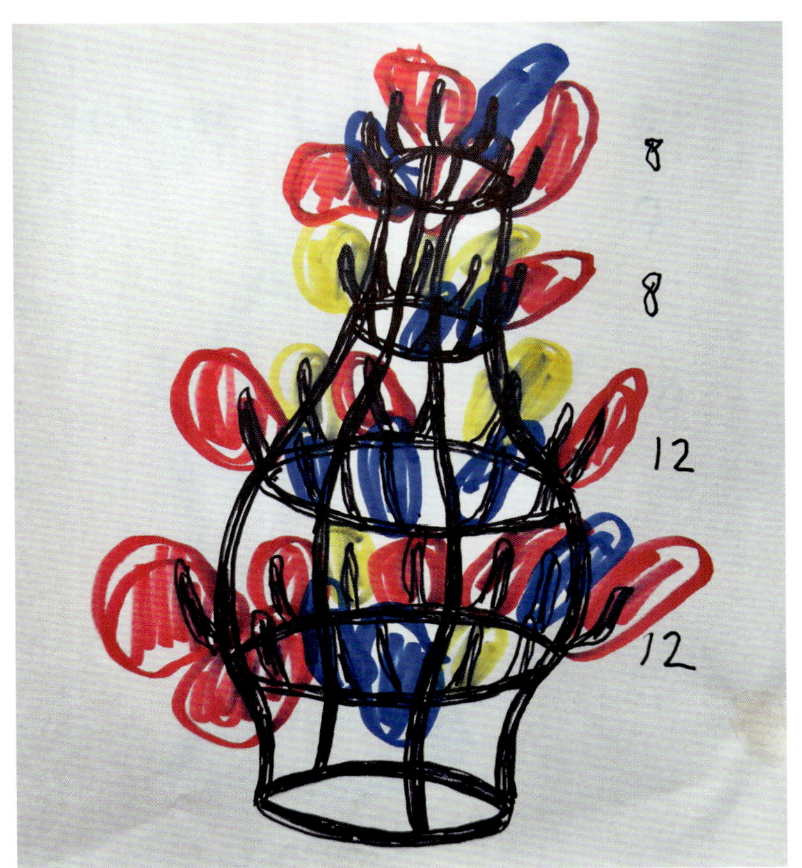

Dokoupil embraces the imperfections and the element of surprise that arise from this technique, challenging the idea of the artist's complete control over the artwork. Furthermore, the bubble paintings also explore the interplay between order and chaos, as the bubbles interact with the preexisting paint on the canvas. The resulting compositions often exhibit a delicate balance between structured forms and spontaneous marks, inviting viewers to contemplate the harmony and tension between control and spontaneity in art making.

In traditional painting techniques, artists exercise a considerable degree of control over their materials, carefully manipulating brushstrokes and color choices. Here, the technique and characteristics of Dokoupil's bubble paintings play a crucial role in their overall aesthetic and conceptual impact. Indeed, bubble paintings introduce an element of surprise and relinquishment of control, as the artist allows the bubbles to create their own unique imprints on the canvas. By embracing the element of surprise, he defies the idea that the artist has complete control over the outcome of their work. This delicate equilibrium invites viewers to contemplate the tension and harmony between control and spontaneity, challenging conventional ideas about the role of the artist in the creation of art.

As mentioned above, Dokoupil's artistic practice is firmly grounded in a deep engagement with art history. Regarding contemporary art, it's fascinating to realize the way he skillfully engages in dialogues with other artists within his works while maintaining a steadfast commitment to his own aristic vision and program. Andy Warhol and Yves Klein are two of his favorites. Each of these artists contributed significantly to the development of modern and contemporary art in their own unique way, and you can feel their fundamental nature to some extent there.

The exhibition in Venice features various large-scale bubble paintings, vitrines containing bubbles on paper, and glass bubble sculptures. Some paintings boast elaborate, colorful abstract backgrounds, while others showcase Fra Angelico's lapis lazuli surfaces behind the bubbles. Additionally, there are paintings that exude a highly expressive quality, while others present a more minimalistic approach.

The brand-new sculptures are a collaborative effort between Dokoupil and Czech glass masters, who were instructed by the artist to utilize their expertise

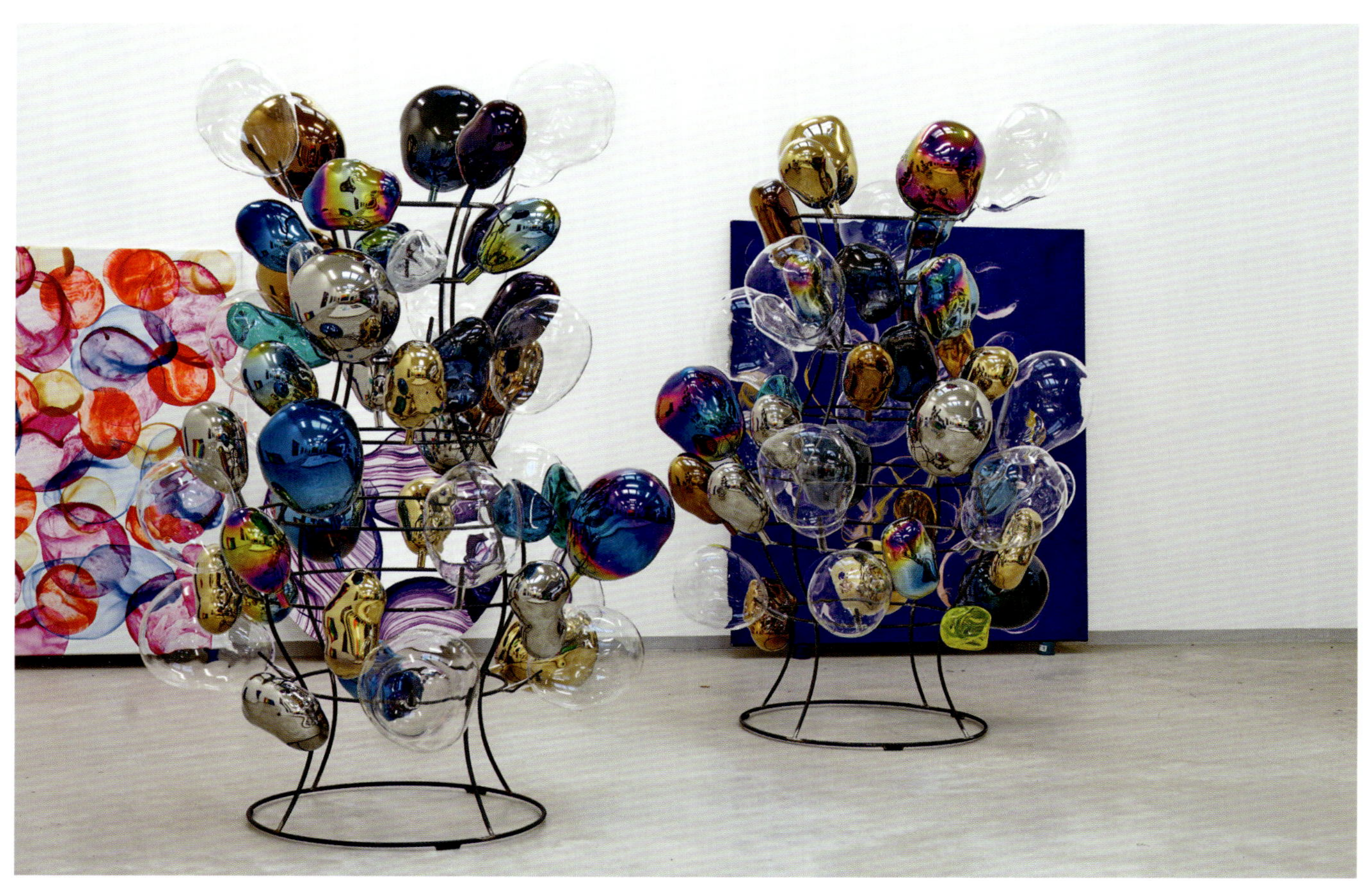

in an opposite manner than they are accustomed to. This direction likely aimed to challenge both the artists' established techniques and the conventional expectations associated with their craftsmanship. Furthermore, by encouraging them to do so, Dokoupil sought to introduce new perspectives and creative dynamics into the sculptural process.

Displaying the glass bubbles in bottle racks reminiscent of those made by Marcel Duchamp serves as a reference to his legacy and subversion of traditional artistic conventions. By doing so, Dokoupil may be drawing a conceptual parallel between his artworks and Duchamp's readymades, suggesting a similar recontextualization of ordinary objects within the realm of art. Nevertheless, I prefer to see a striking visual contrast that exhibits the juxtaposition between fragility and strength, underscoring themes present in Dokoupil's artwork, such as the interplay between transience and permanence.

The recent bubble sculptures evoke the idea of inflating and deflating, resembling balloons being filled with air and released, similarly to Jeff Koons's sculptures. In Peter Sloterdijk's work *Spheres*, the mention of a boy insufflating his breath into bubbles and letting it go suggests a connection to the act of breathing and beyond that to self-determination. Furthermore, Piero Manzoni's *Artist's Breath* serves as a provocative exploration of the artist's own bodily presence and the act of breathing as a fundamental aspect of human existence. Some of us may be tempted to independently focus on visual similarities between Jiri Dokoupil's glass bubbles, but the truth is that each one brings his own unique program. Resemblances and connections should be seen much more as coincidental.

The significance of the new bubble sculptures lies in their ability to encapsulate the essence and vitality of the bubbles depicted in Dokoupil's paintings. Serving as a tangible three-dimensional manifestation of his artistic vision, these sculptures offer viewers a unique opportunity to interact with the artwork on a deeper level. Through exploring their form, texture, and spatial relationships, viewers are invited to uncover layers of complexity and nuance, evoking a sense of mystery and contemplation. This multifaceted engagement encourages viewers to reflect further on the intricate contrasts and complexities inherent in both artistic practice and human existence, enriching their interpretation and experience of Dokoupil's work.

Finally, I want to mention that the works on paper displayed in the vitrines are the result of being placed close to paintings during their execution. Nonetheless, they are certainly not a collateral extension of the paintings. The artist selects certain pieces based on specific interests and later combines them in the vitrines according to his artistic criteria.

"We build too many walls and not enough bridges." – Isaac Newton

"BUBBLES ARE THE ANSWER TO EVERYTHING"

Jiri Georg Dokoupil

EVERYTHING
I KNOW AND
I THINK OF

BECOMES A

BUBBLE.

I KNEW THAT
IN ORDER TO BECOME
THE BEST PAINTER
IN THE WORLD,
I   HAD TO
CHANGE MY TECHNOLOGY
— ONLY THIS WAY
WOULD I ACHIEVE NEW
VISUAL RESULTS. I
WAS SUCCESFUL I
BECAME THE BEST
BUBBLE-PAINTER IN THE
              WORLD.

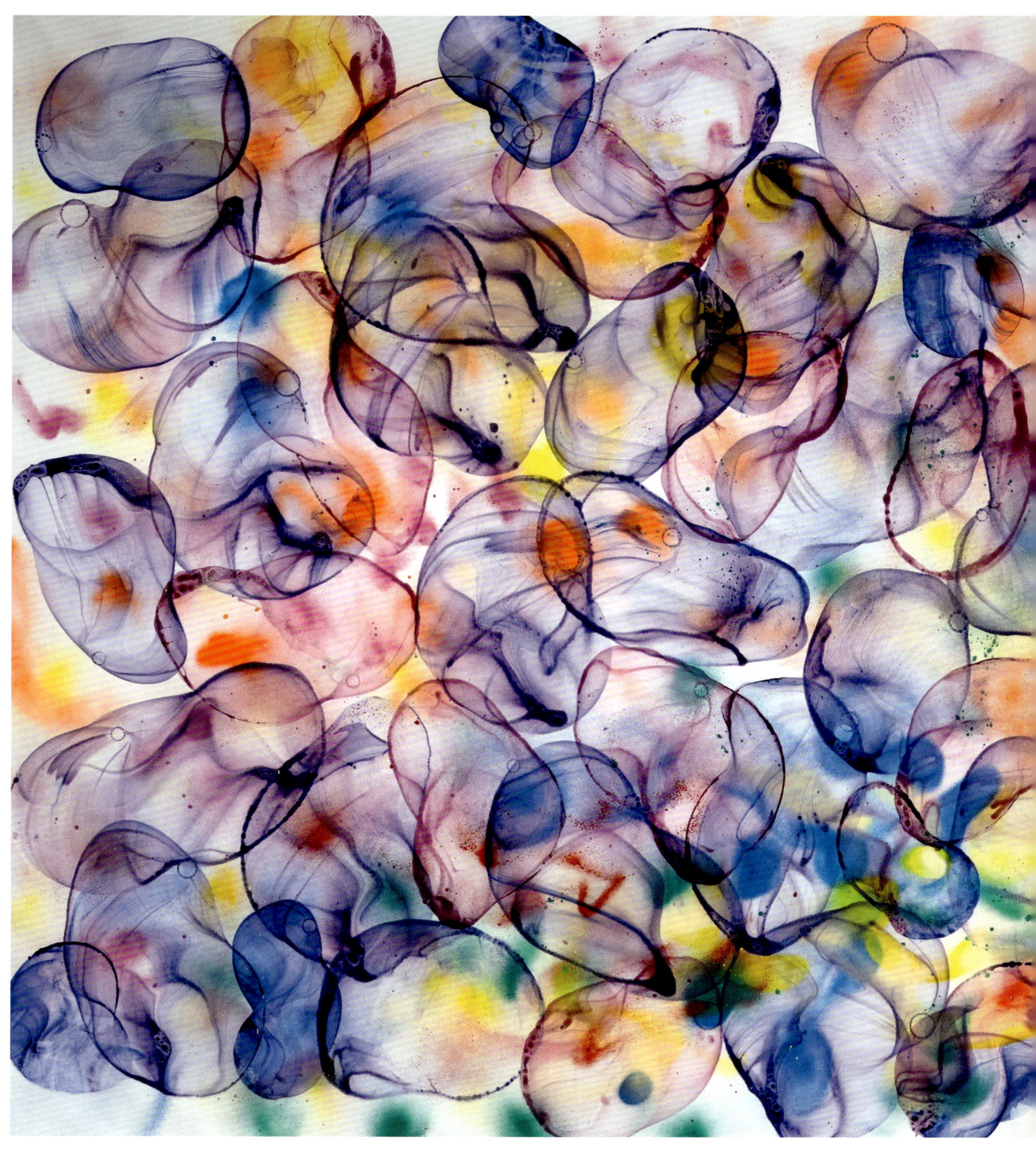

Egun On (Buenos Dias), 2023
Soap-lye and pigments on canvas
205 × 390 cm

Pages 38–39
Untitled, 2023
Soap-lye and pigments on canvas
245 × 390 cm

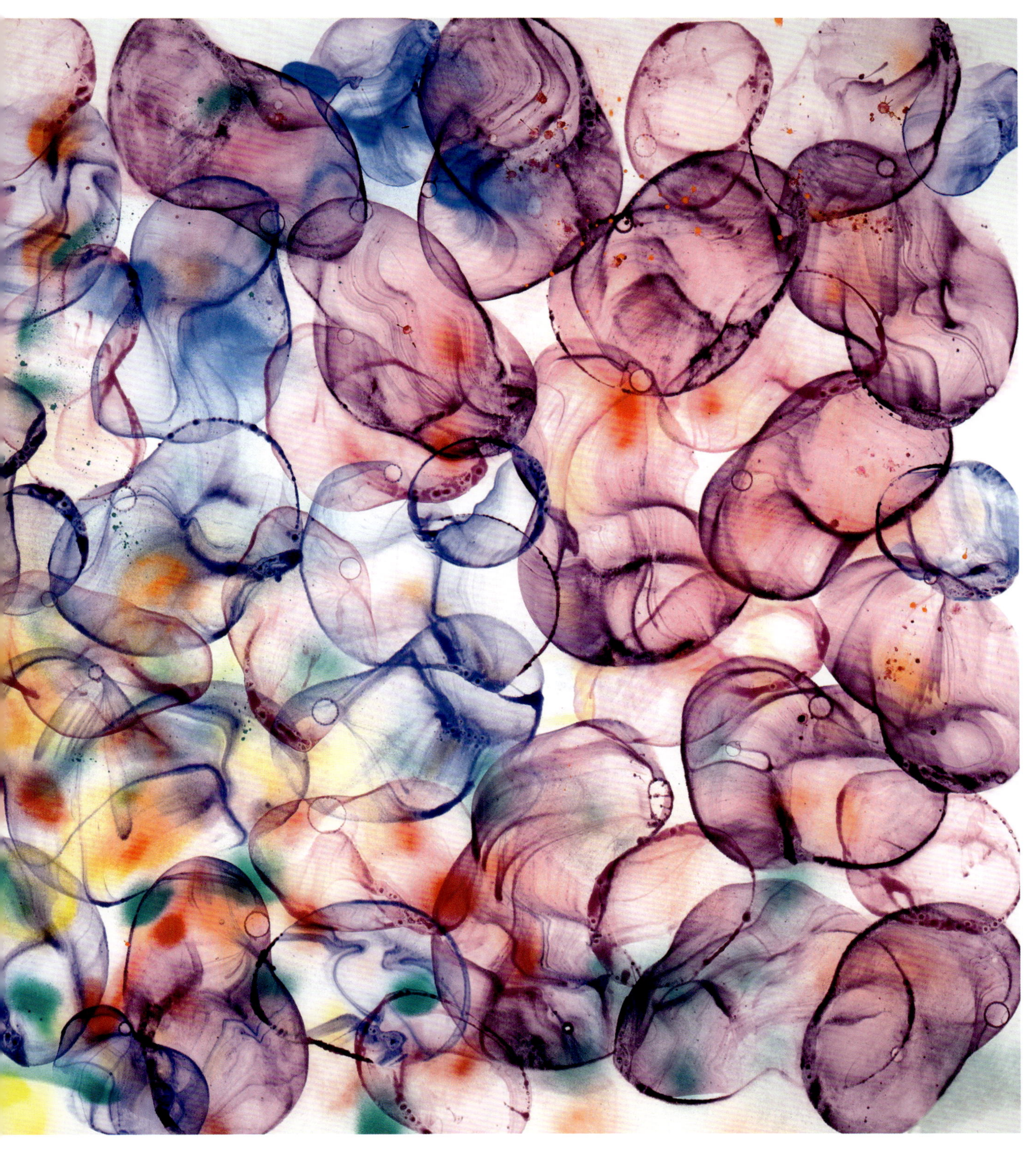

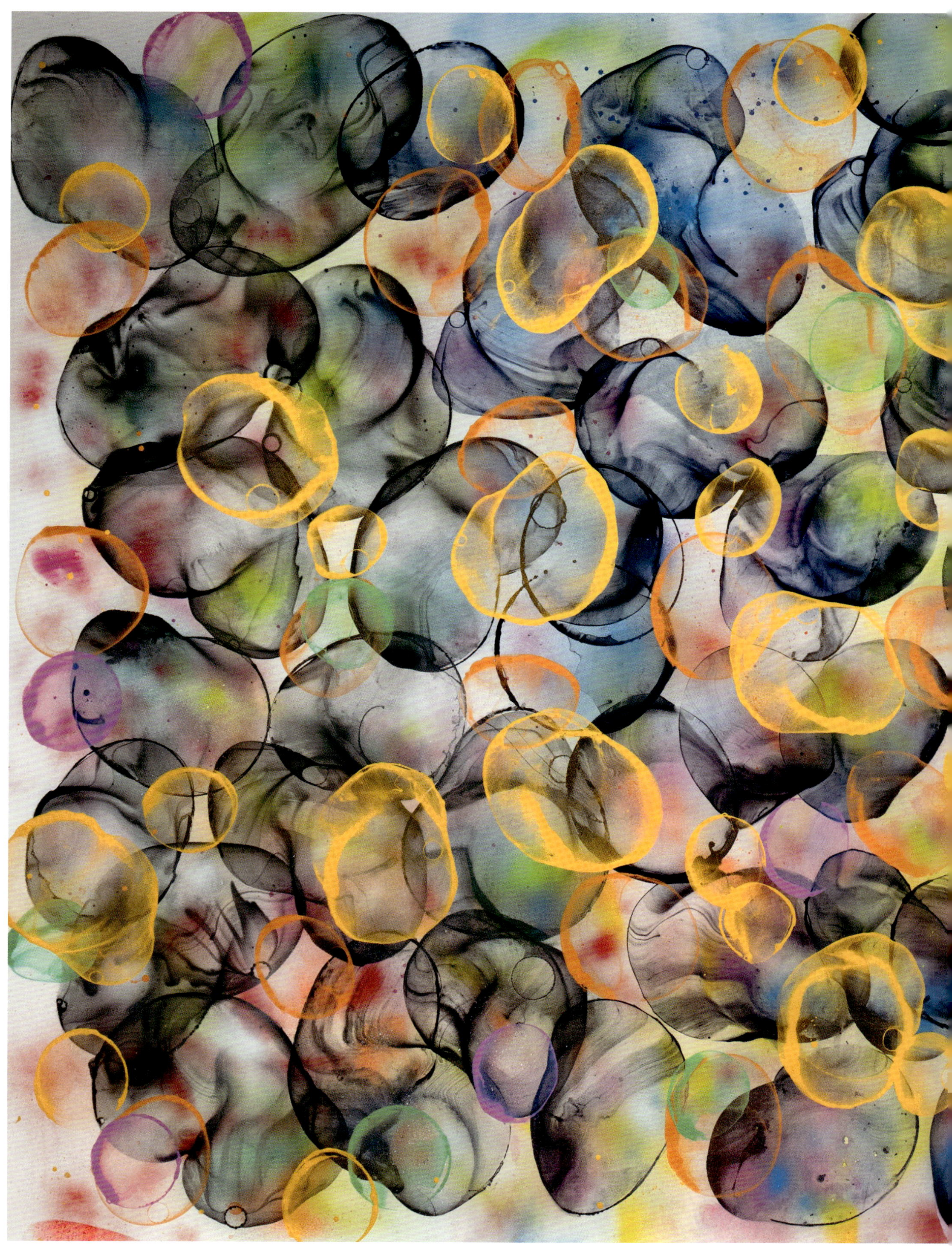

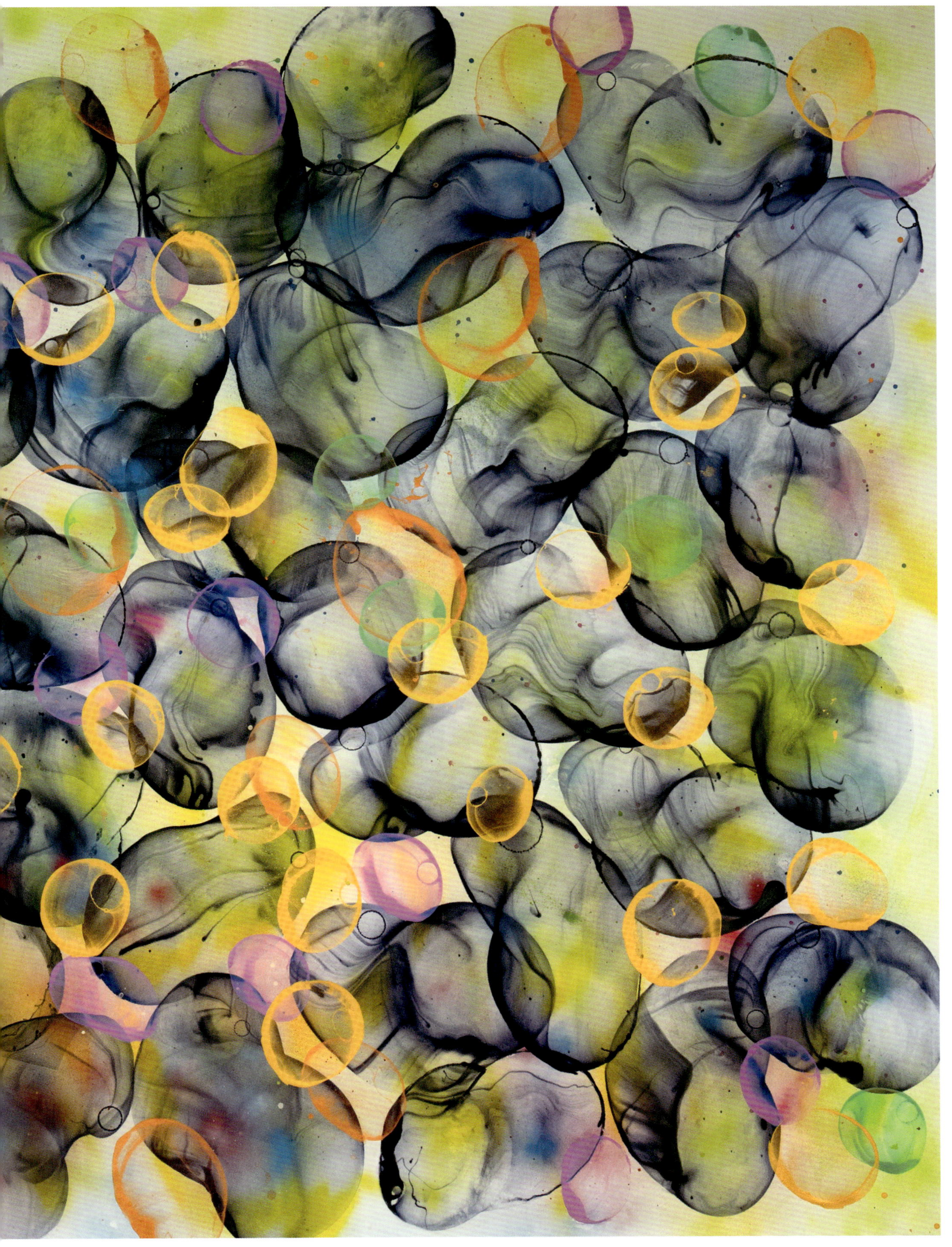

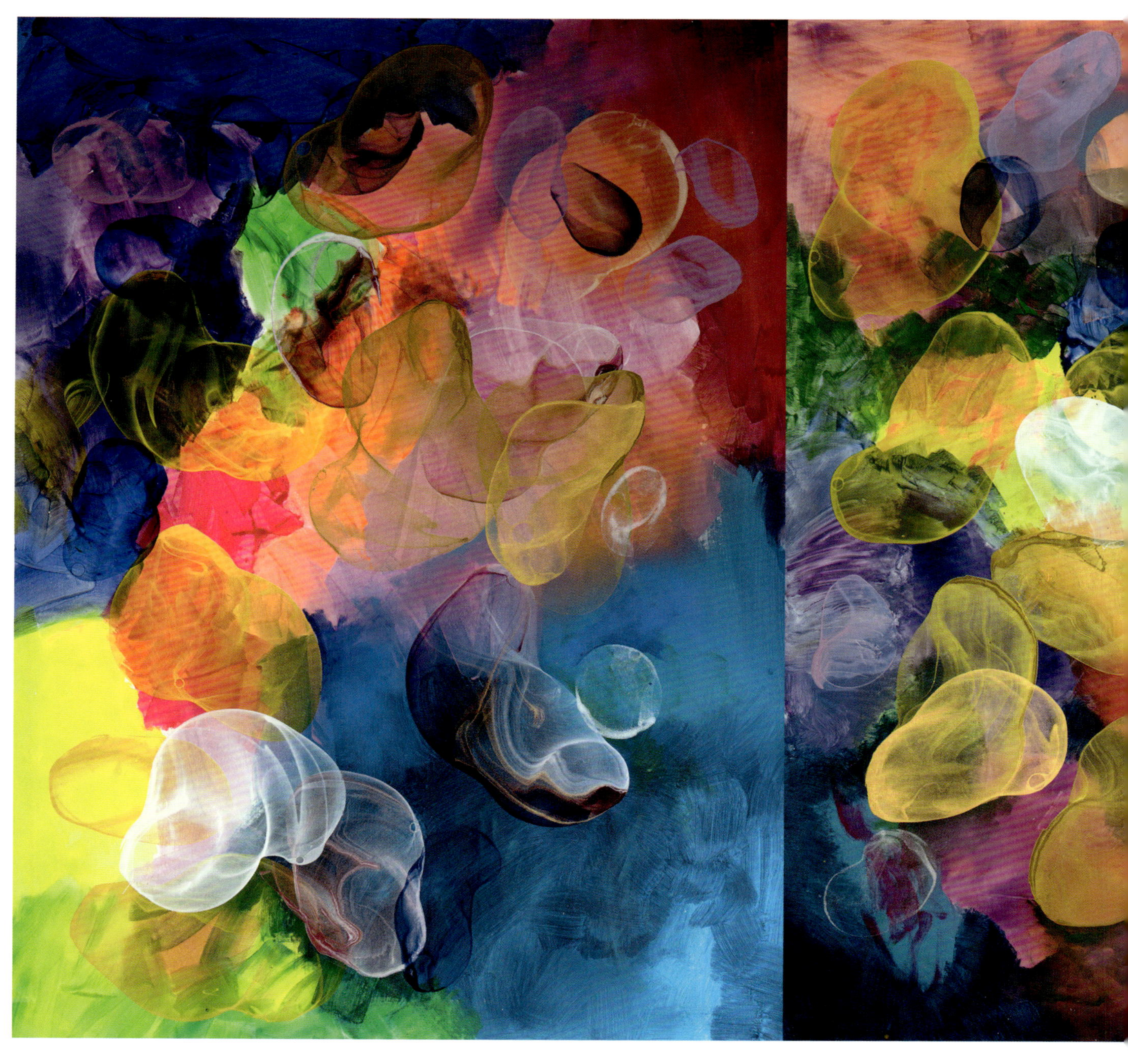

Chinese Triptych, 2018–20
Soap-lye and pigments on canvas
205 × 465 cm

Pages 42–43
Bubble Frame, 2018
Soap-lye and pigments on canvas
205 × 300 cm

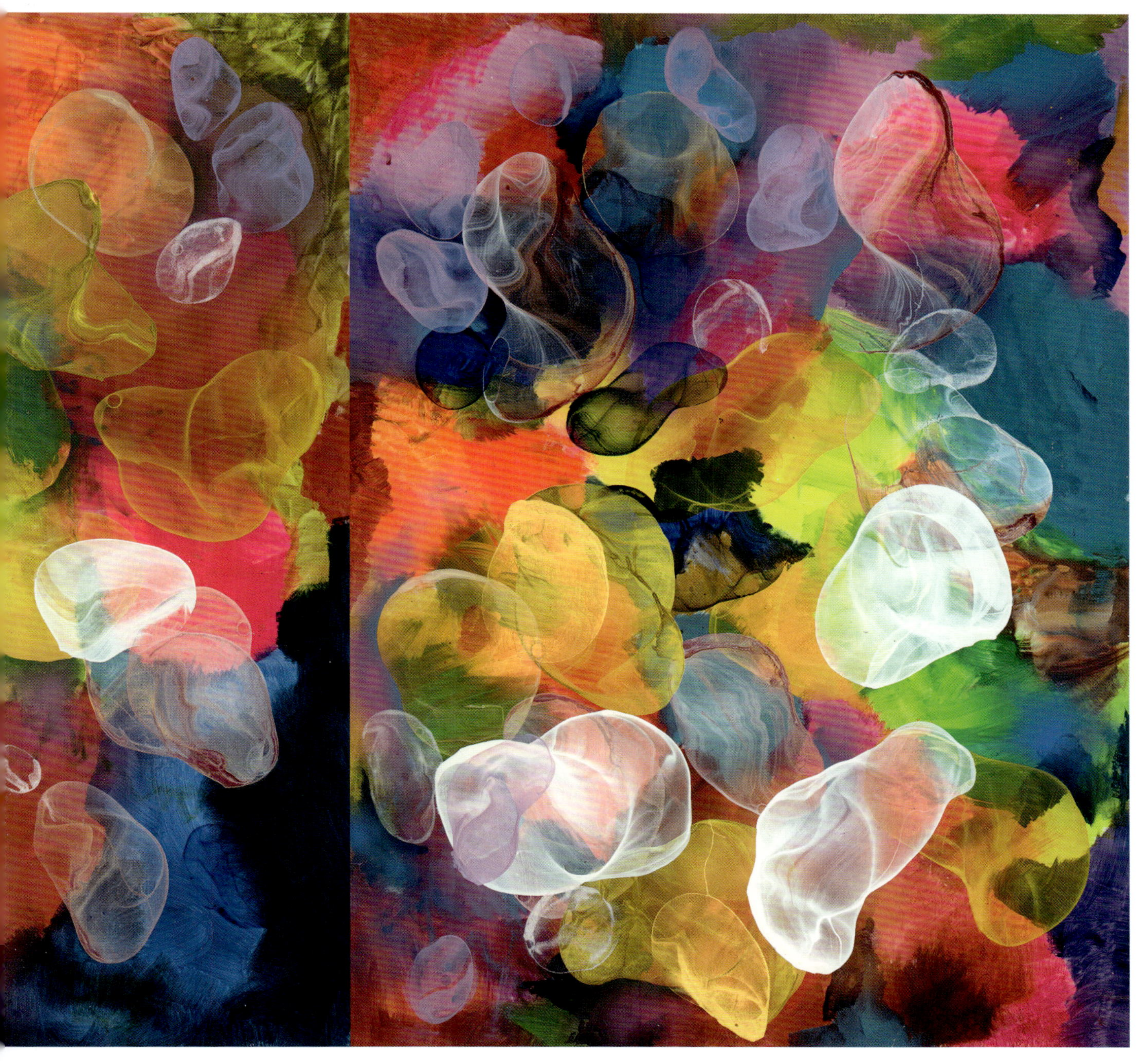

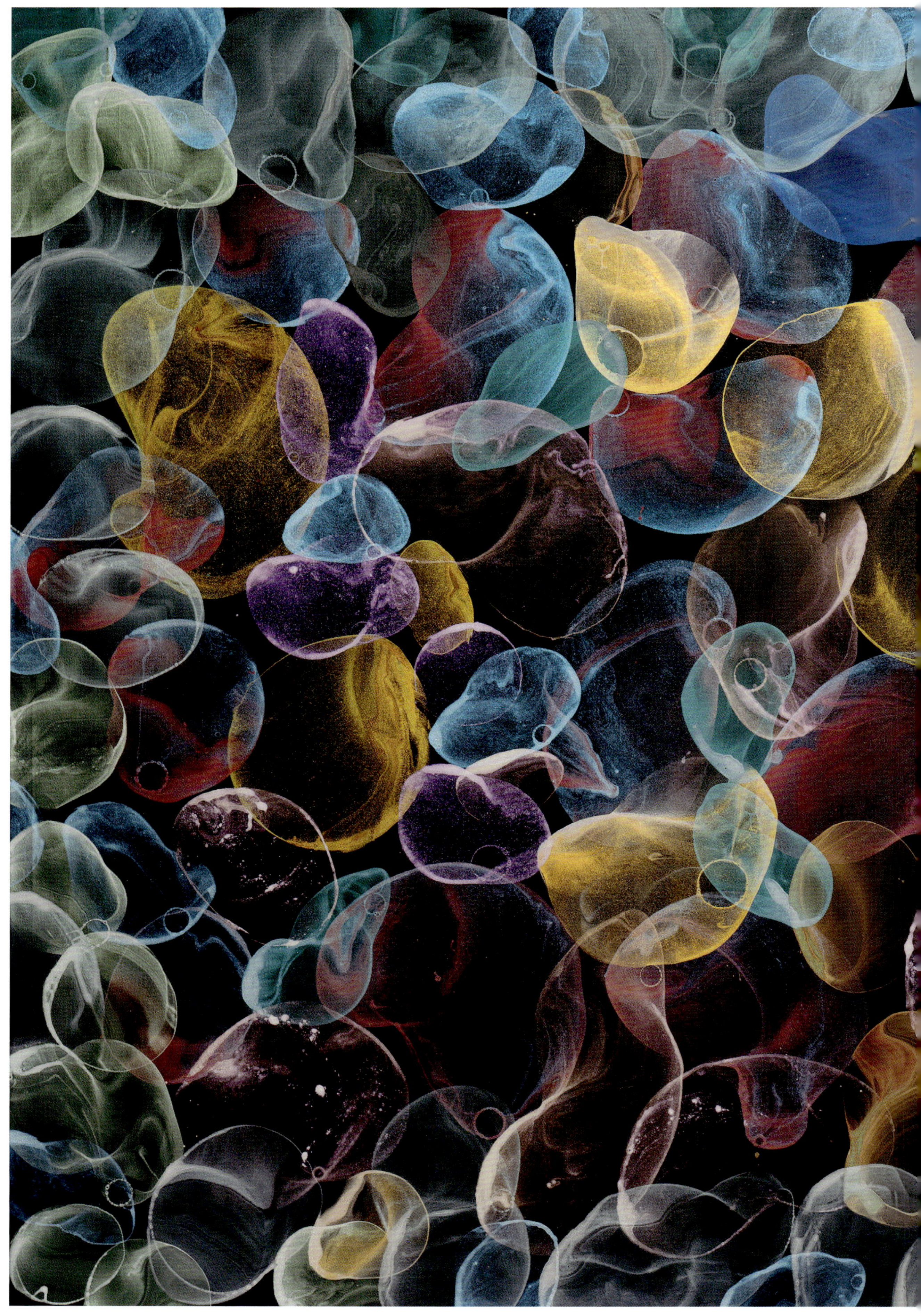

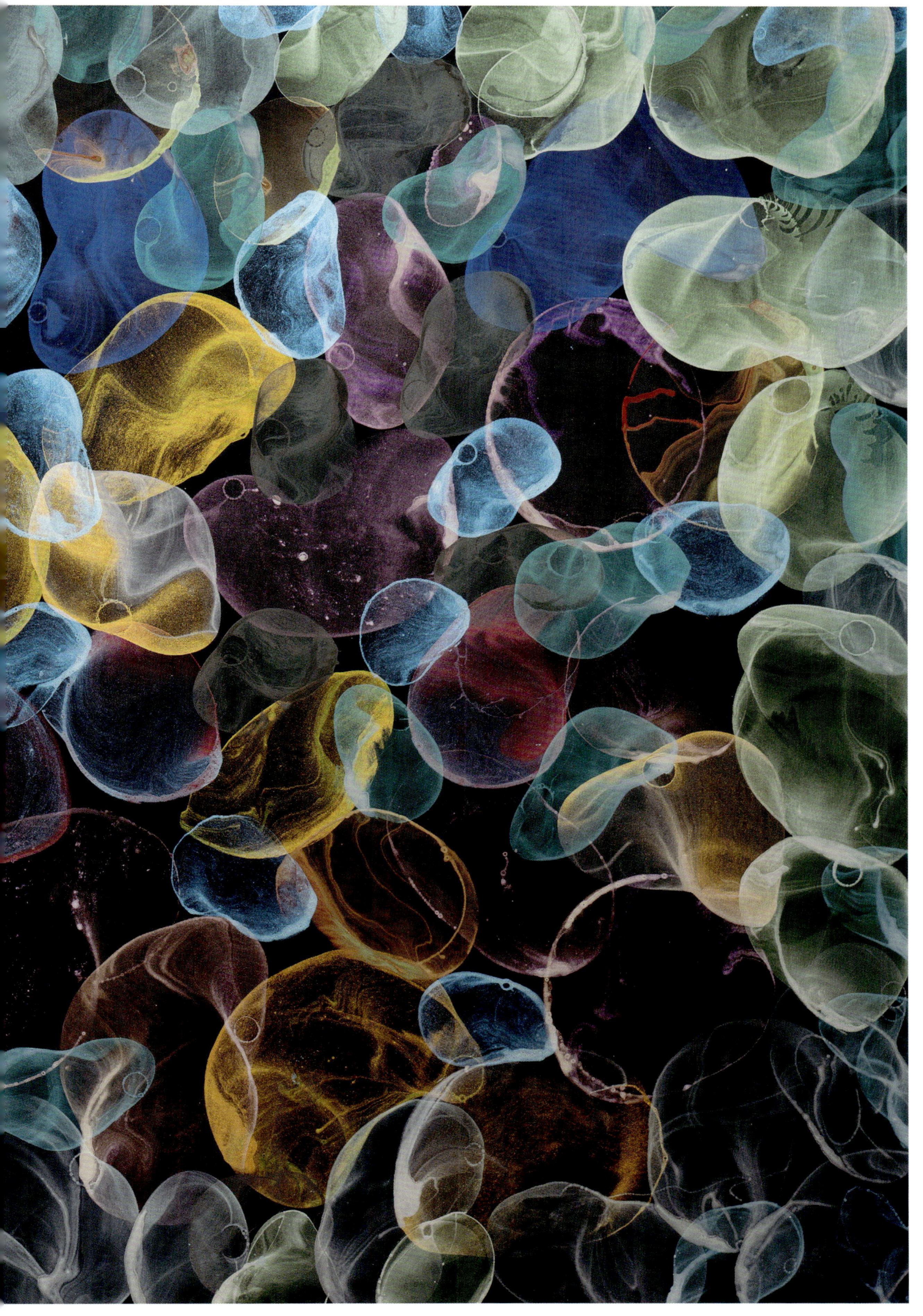

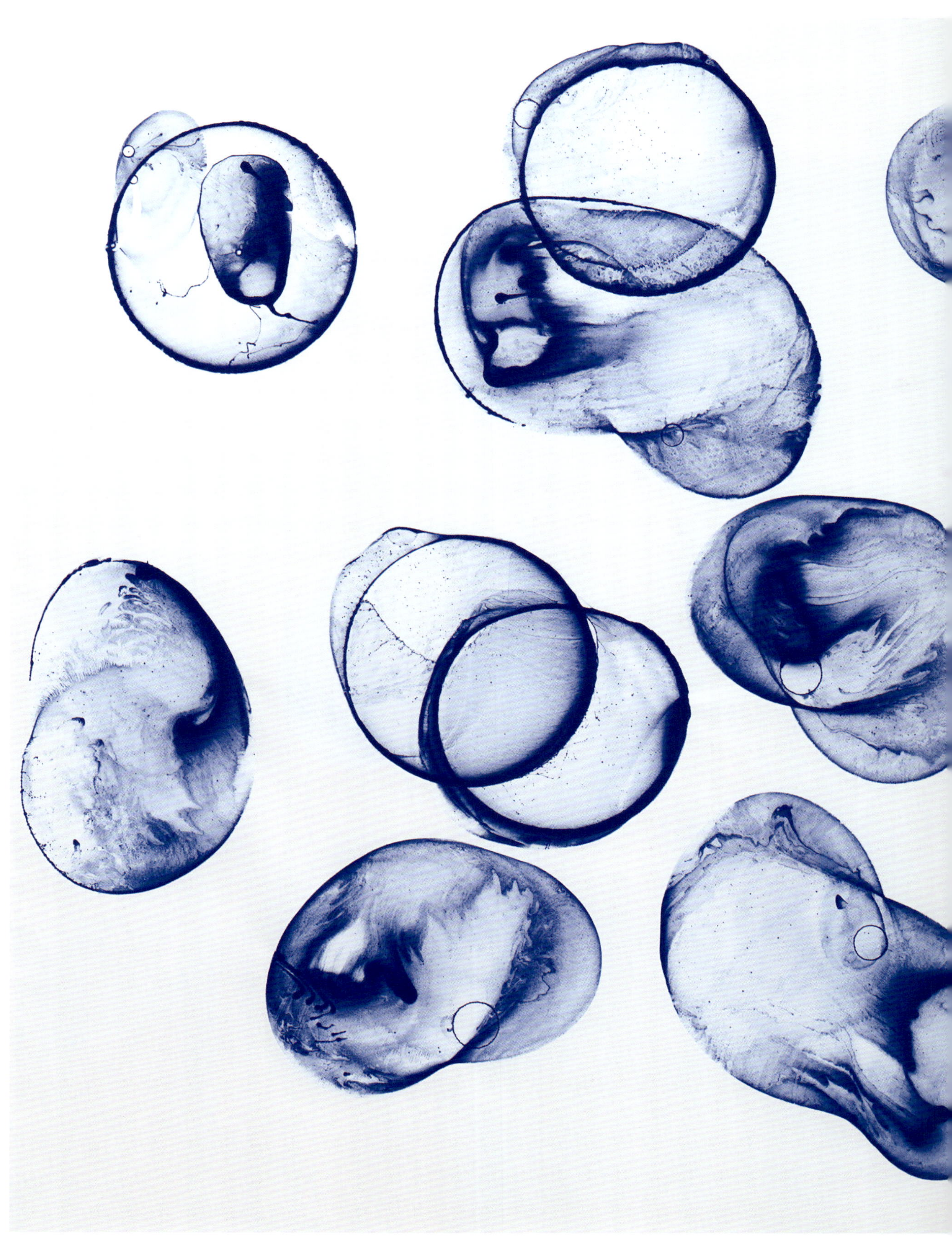

Weiß-Blau, 2022–23
Soap-lye and pigments on canvas
245 × 400 cm

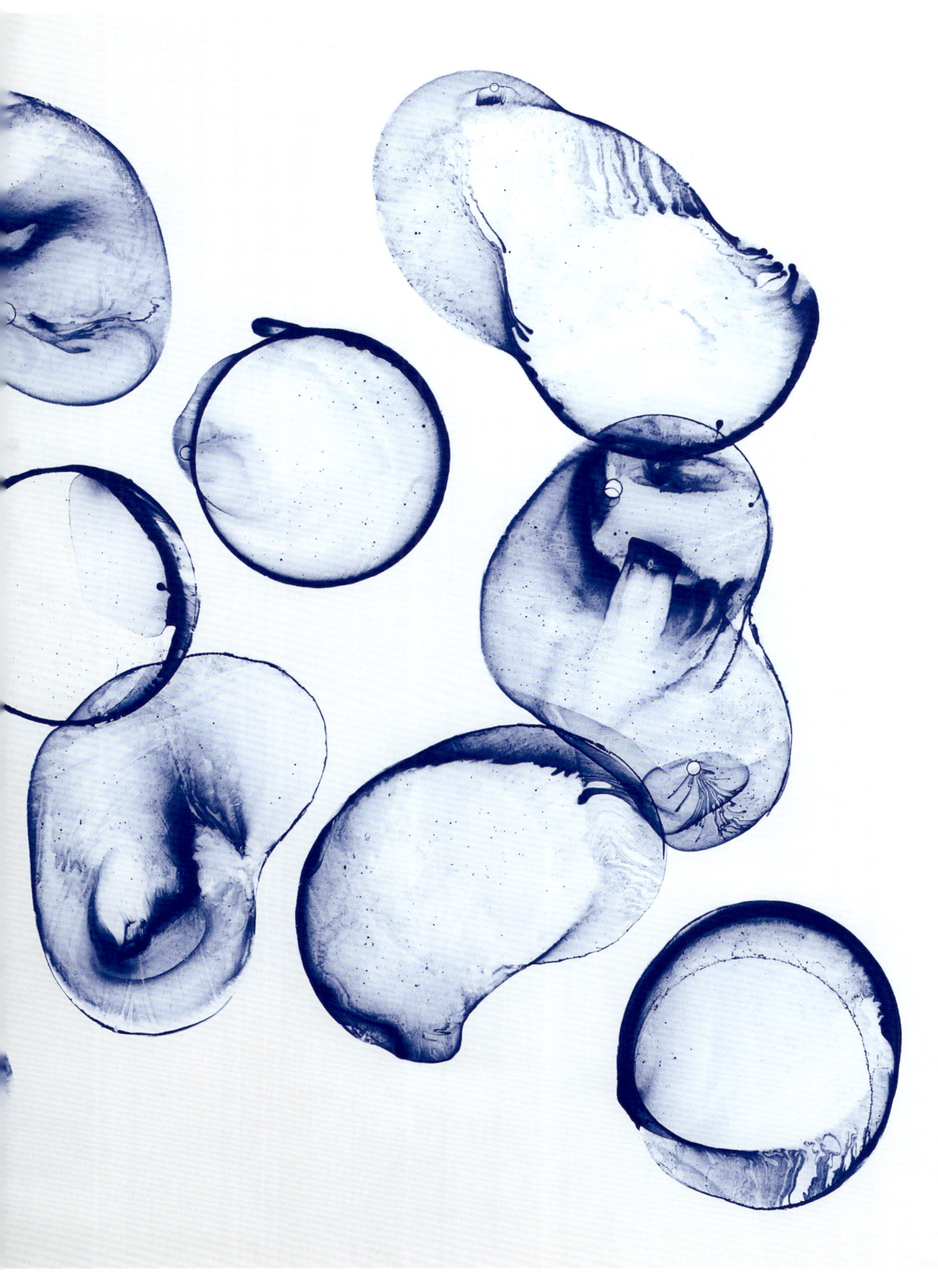

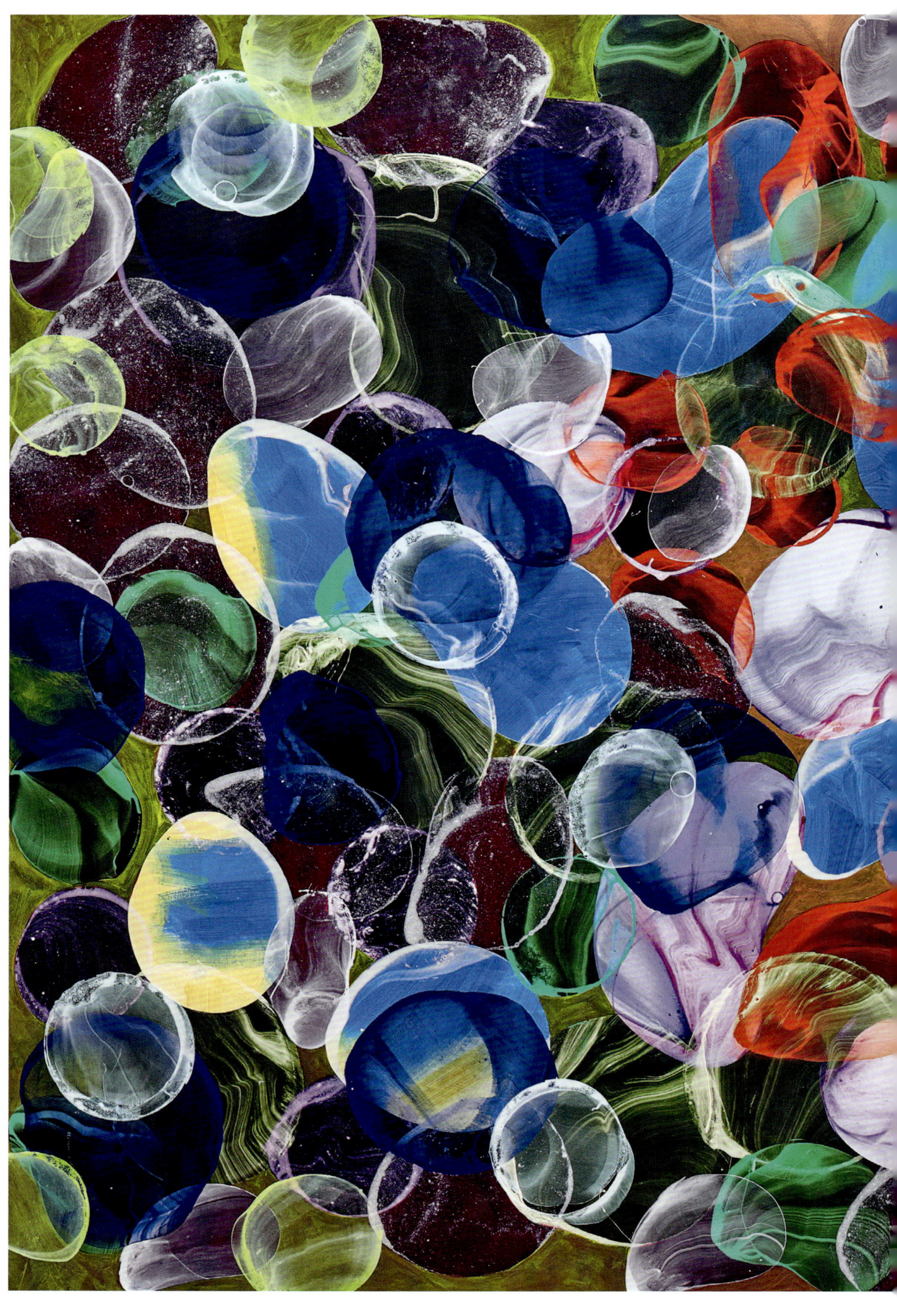

Battle I, 2023
Soap-lye and pigments on canvas
205 × 300 cm

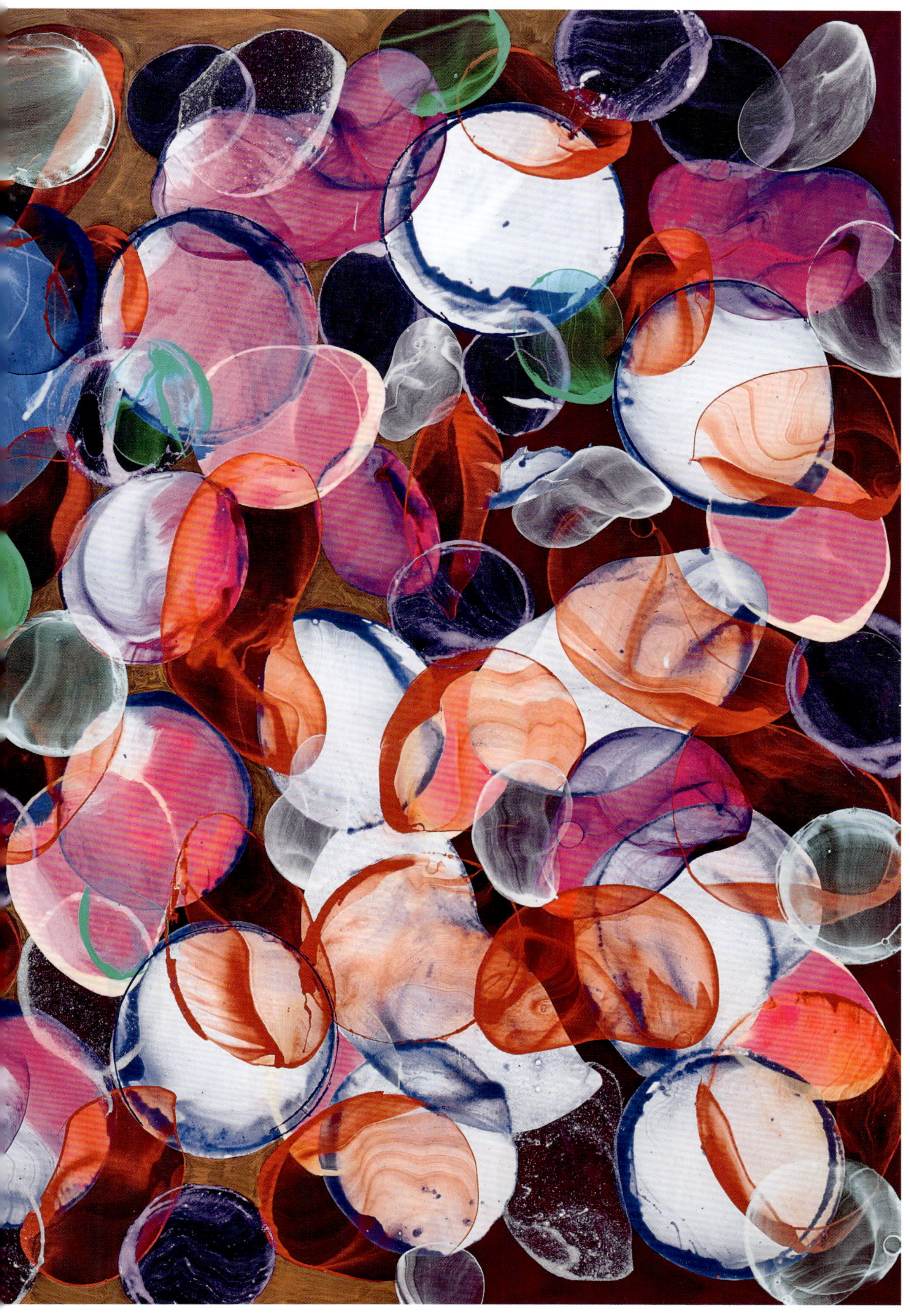

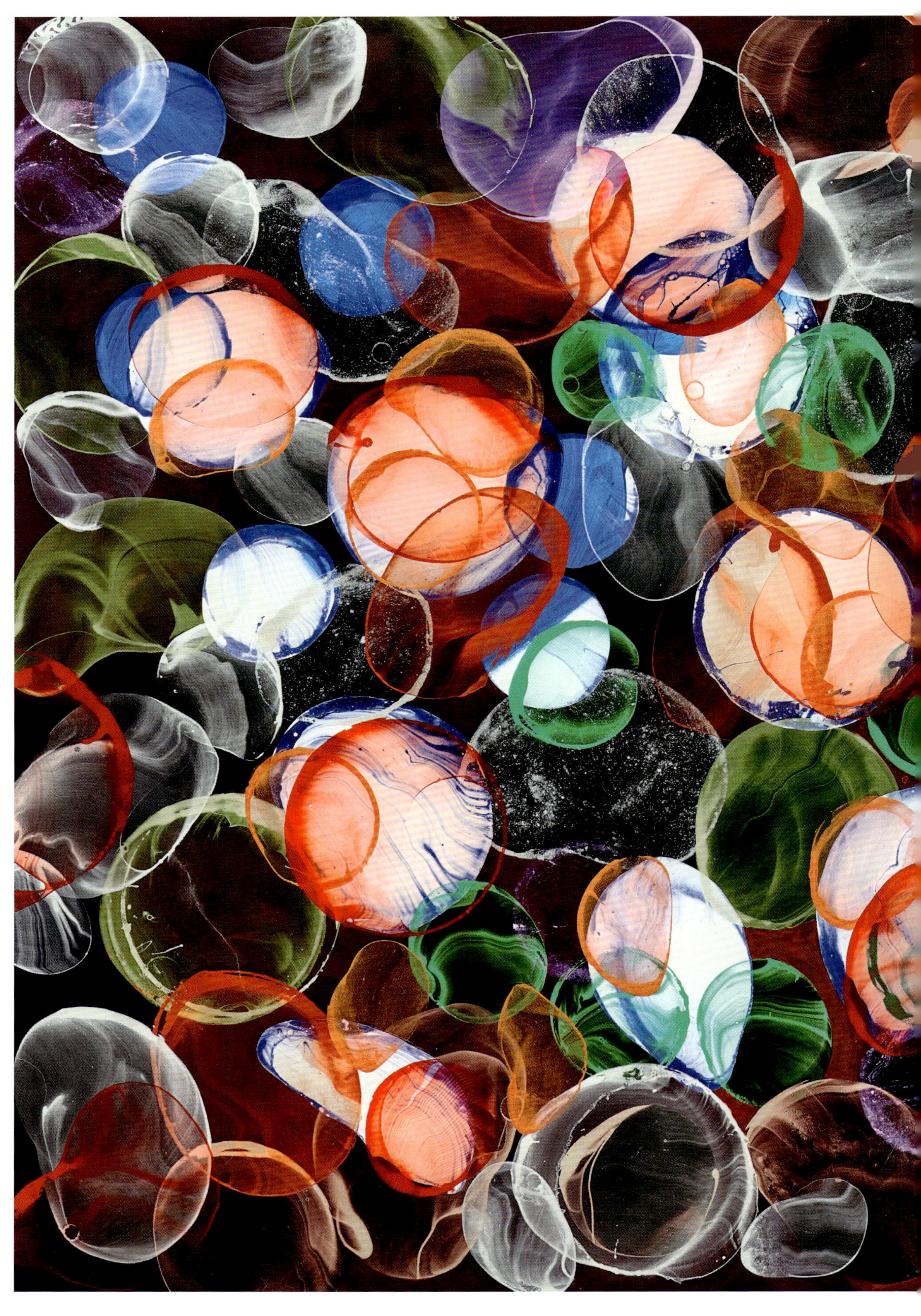

Battle III, 2023
Soap-lye and pigments on canvas
205 × 300 cm

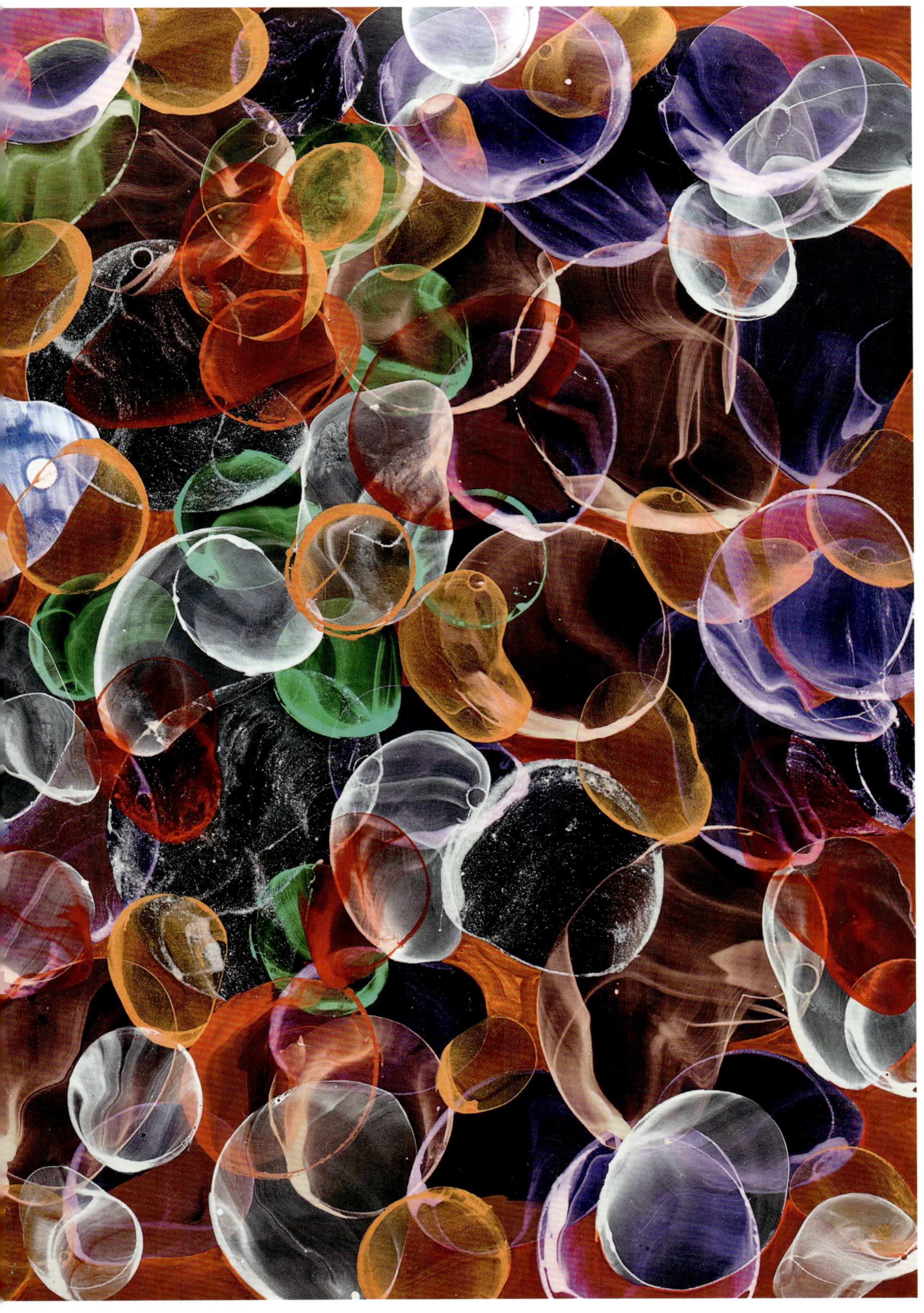

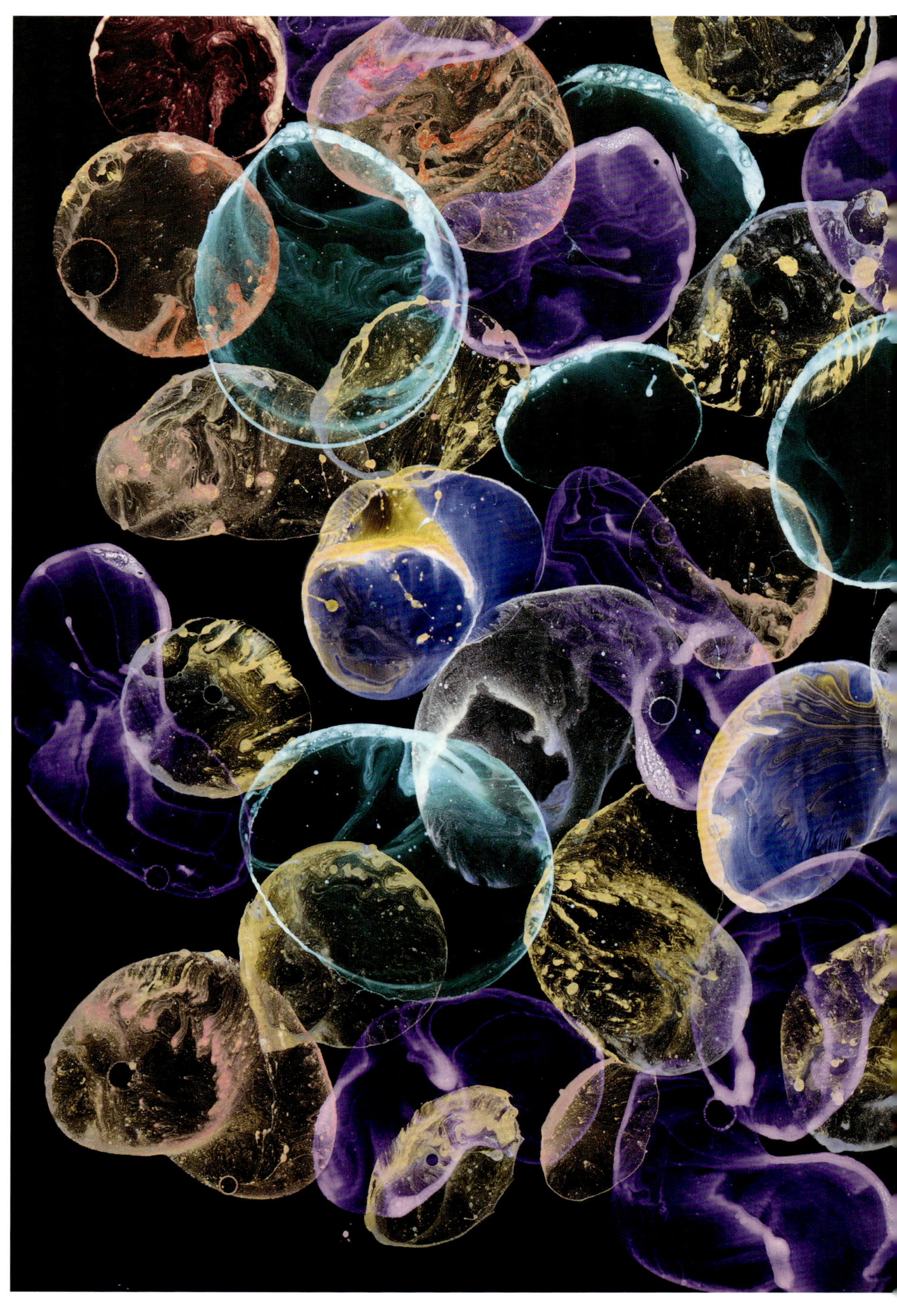

Untitled, 2023
Soap-lye and pigments on canvas
205 × 300 cm

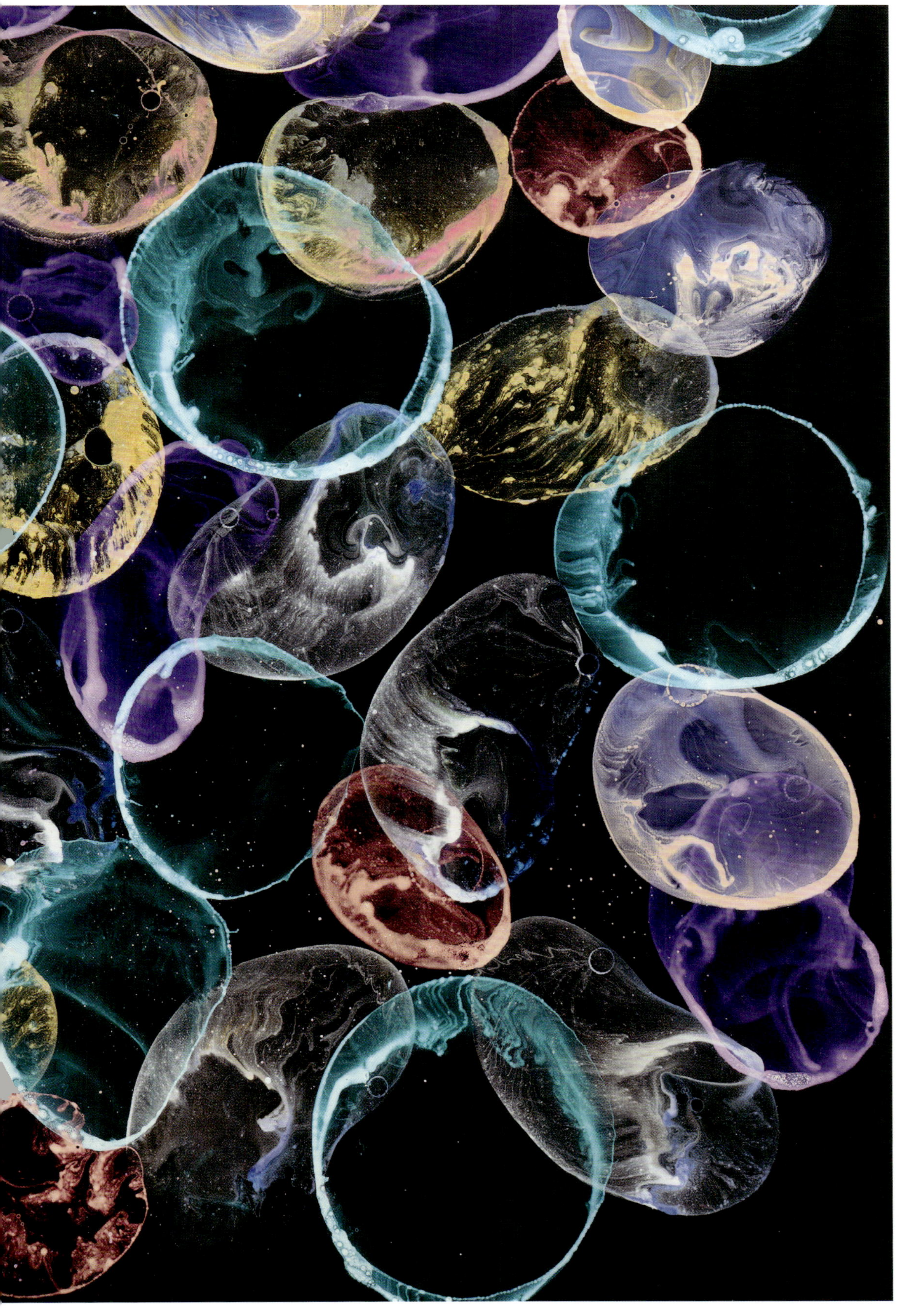

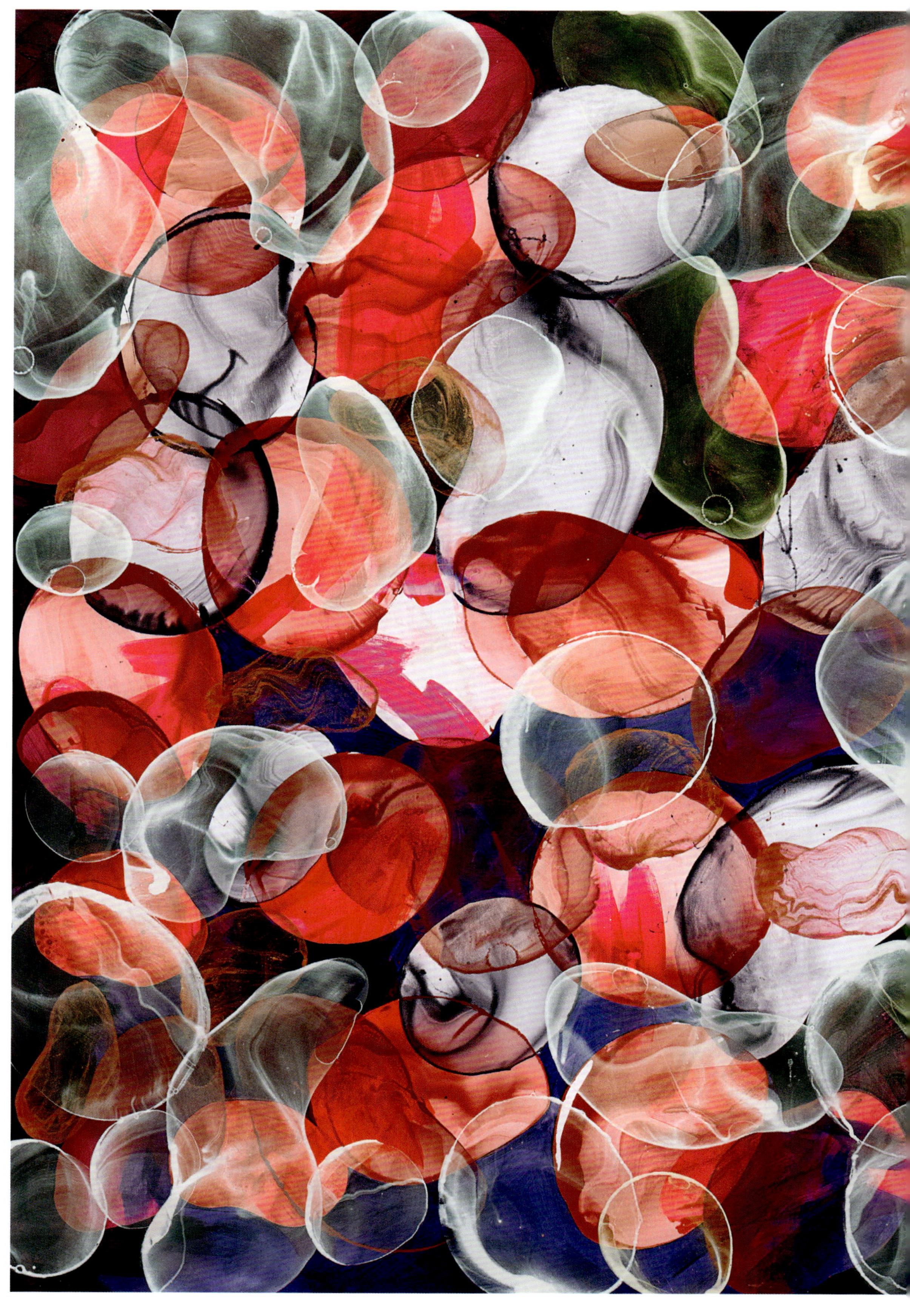

Battle II, 2023
Soap-lye and pigments on canvas
205 × 300 cm

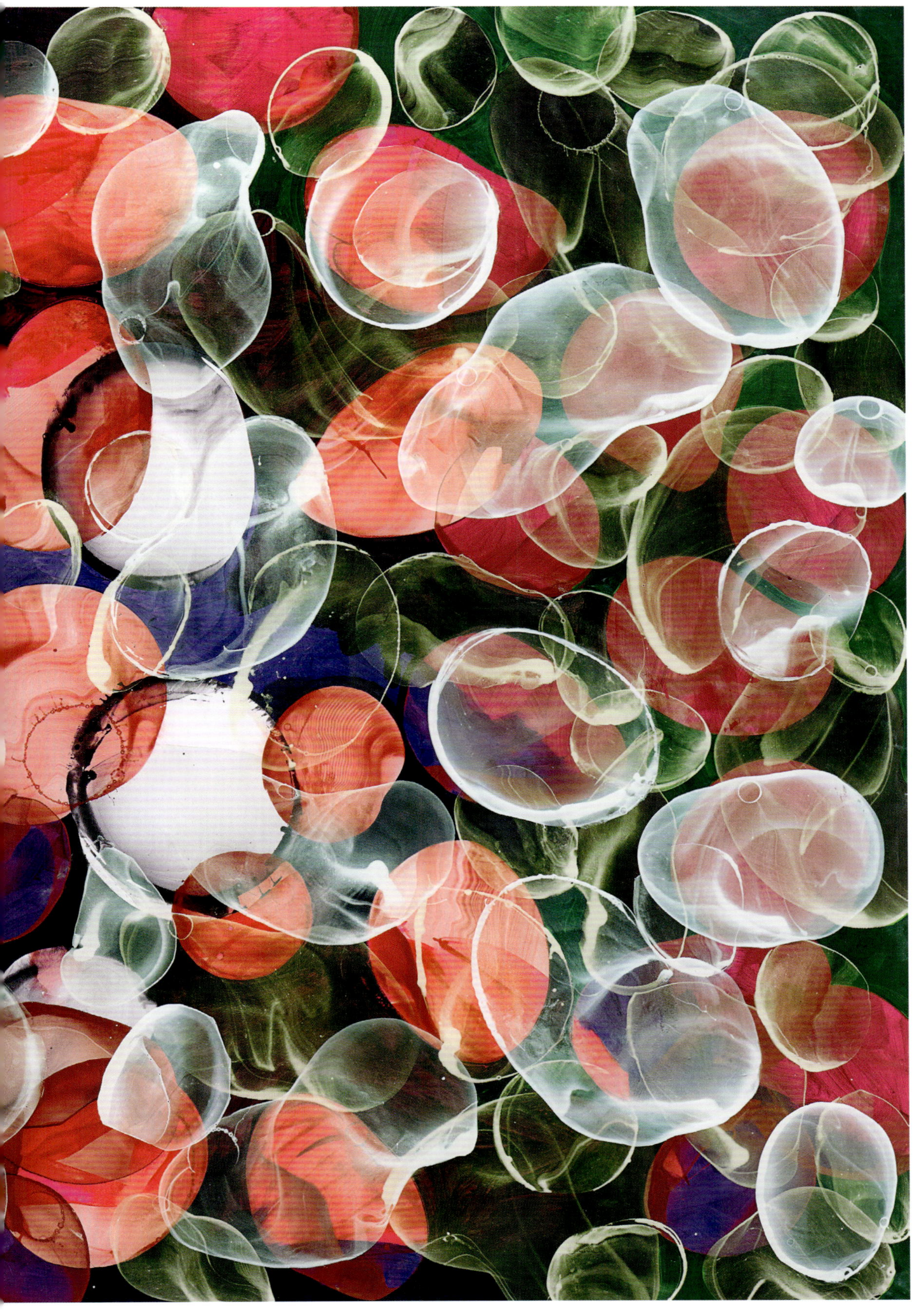

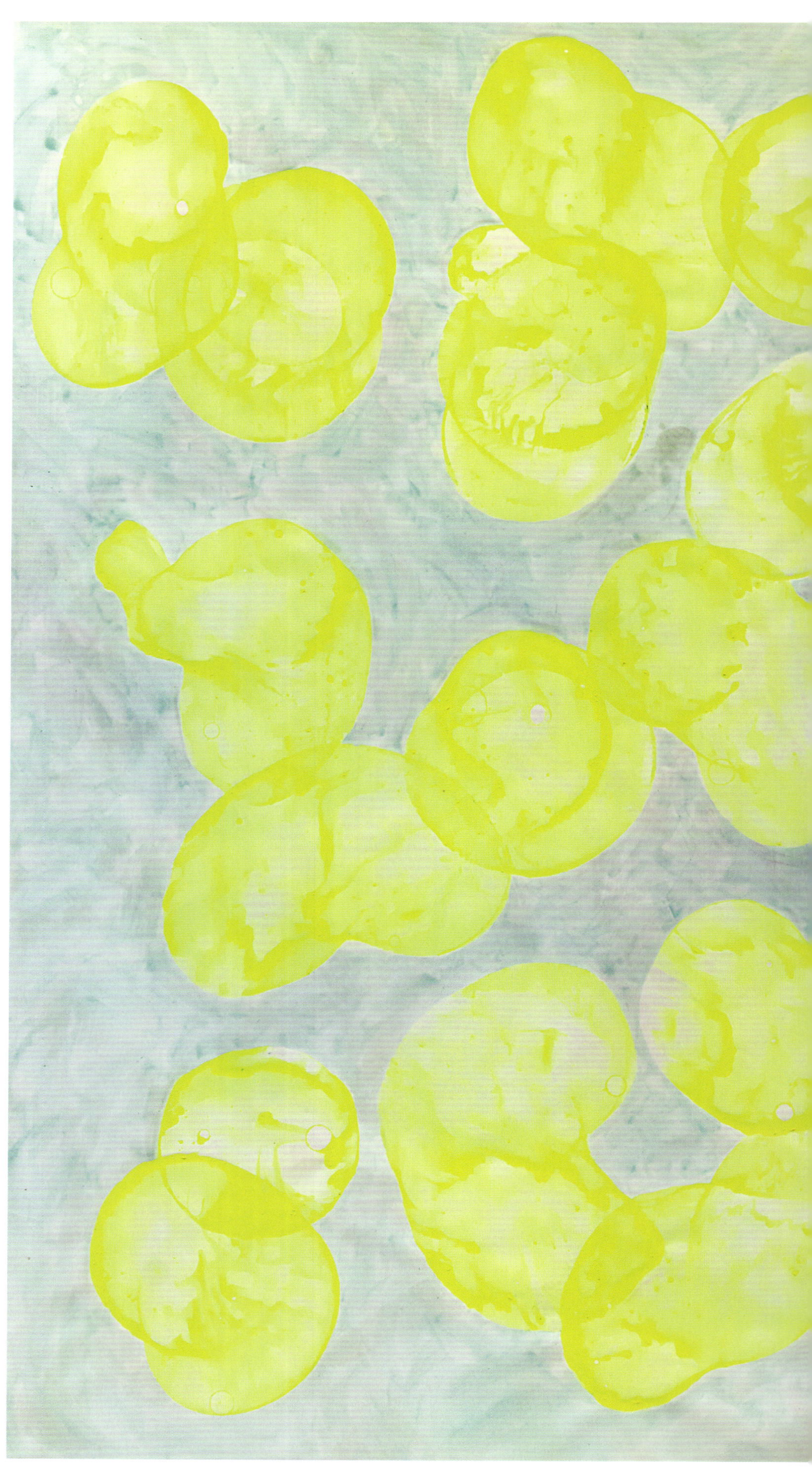

Untitled, 2024
Soap-lye and pigments on canvas
245 × 290 cm

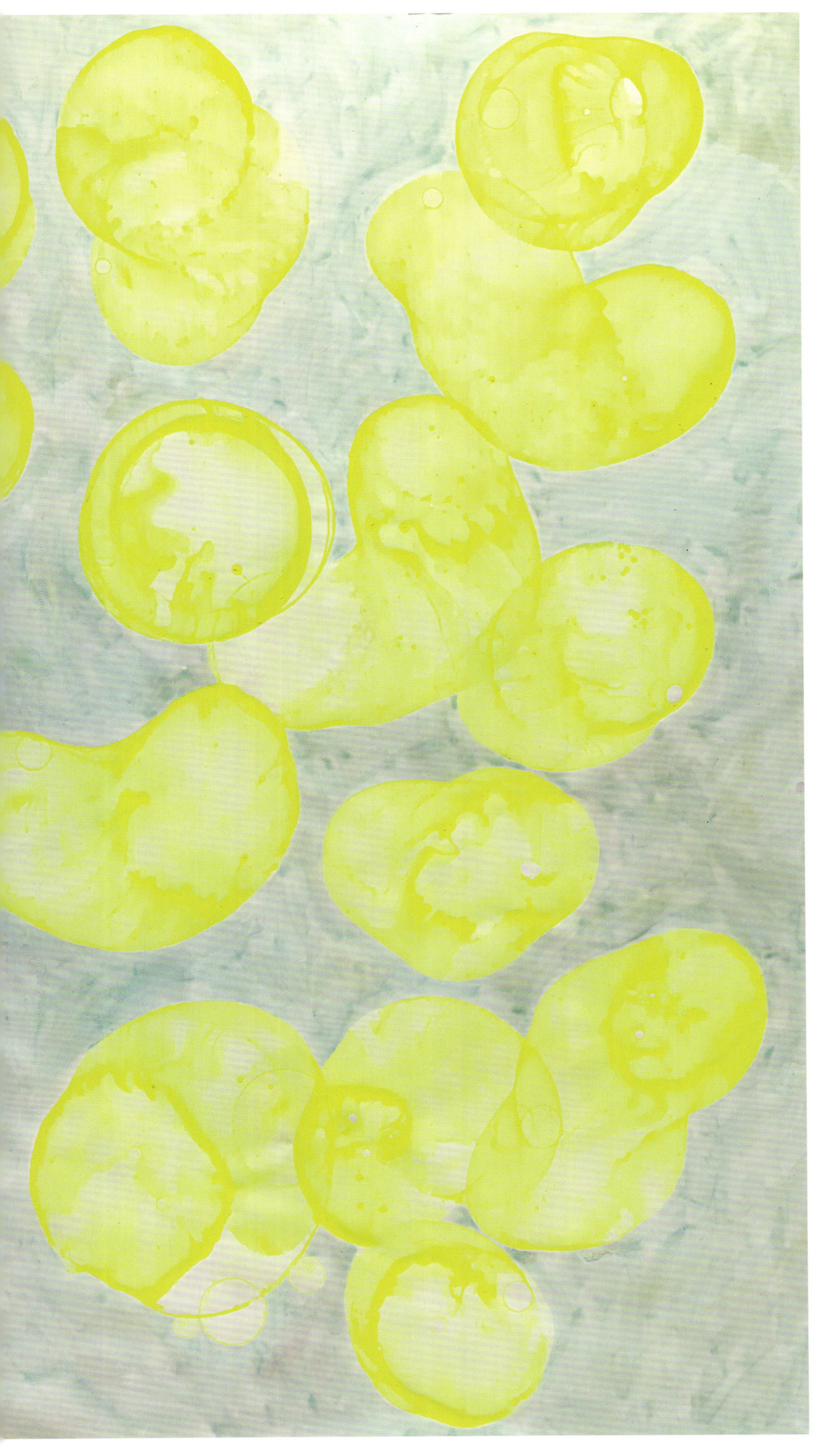

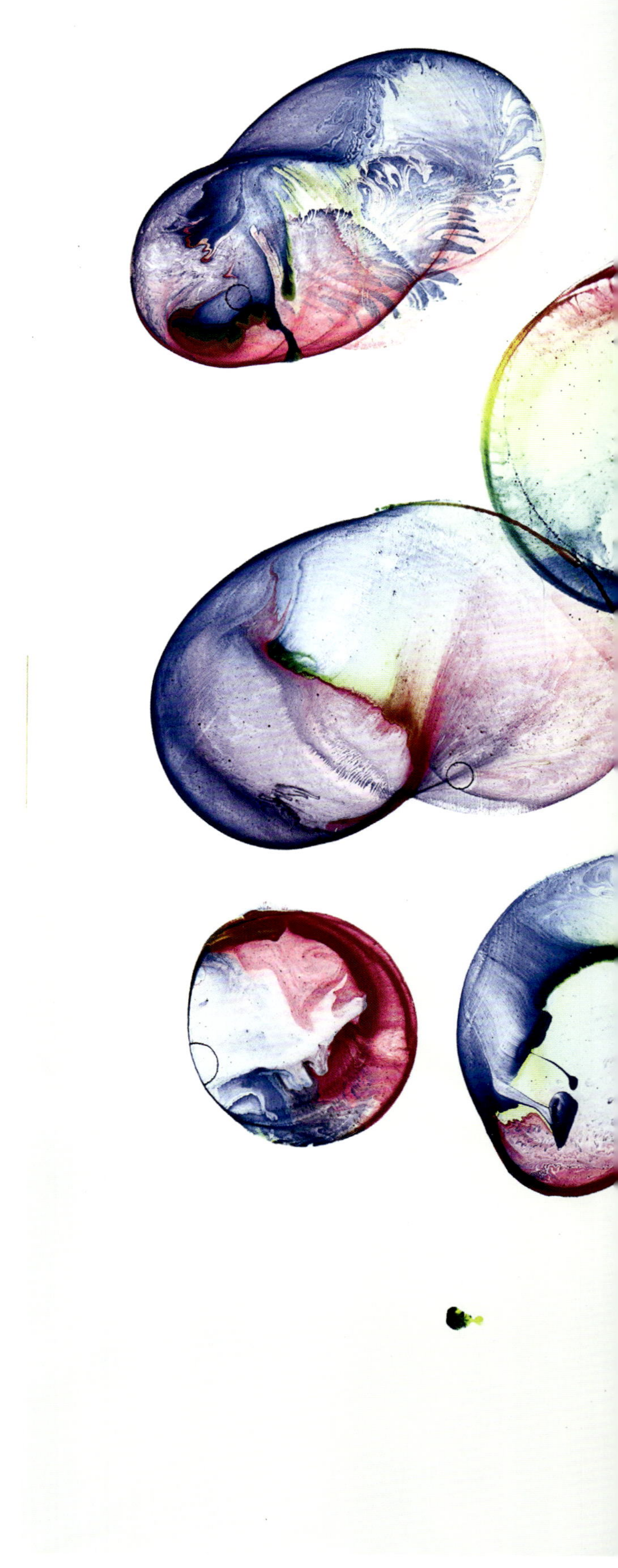

Untitled, 2024
Soap-lye and pigments on canvas
245 × 290 cm

Pages 58–59
Blau-Gold, 2024
Soap-lye and pigments on canvas
245 × 400 cm

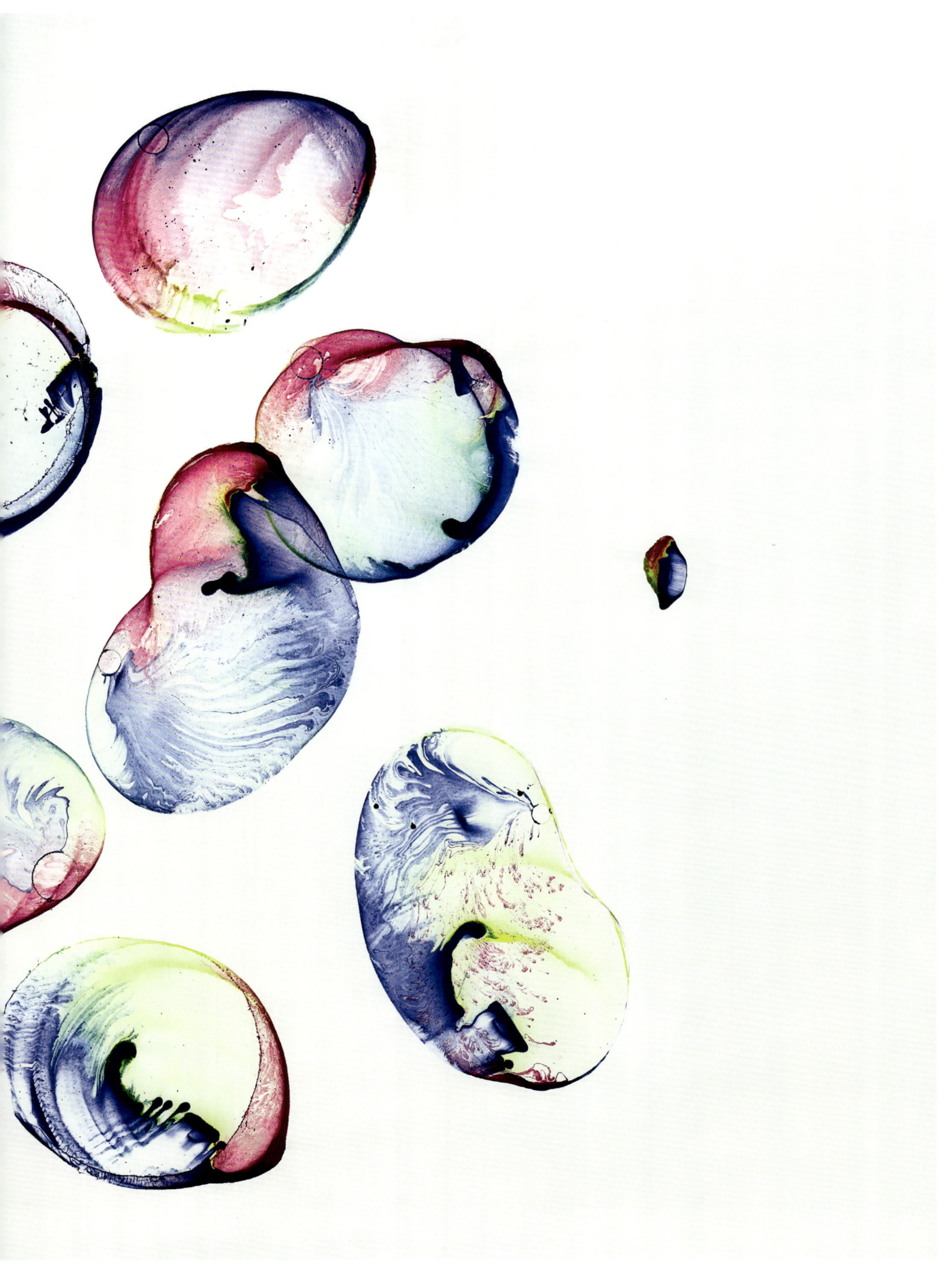

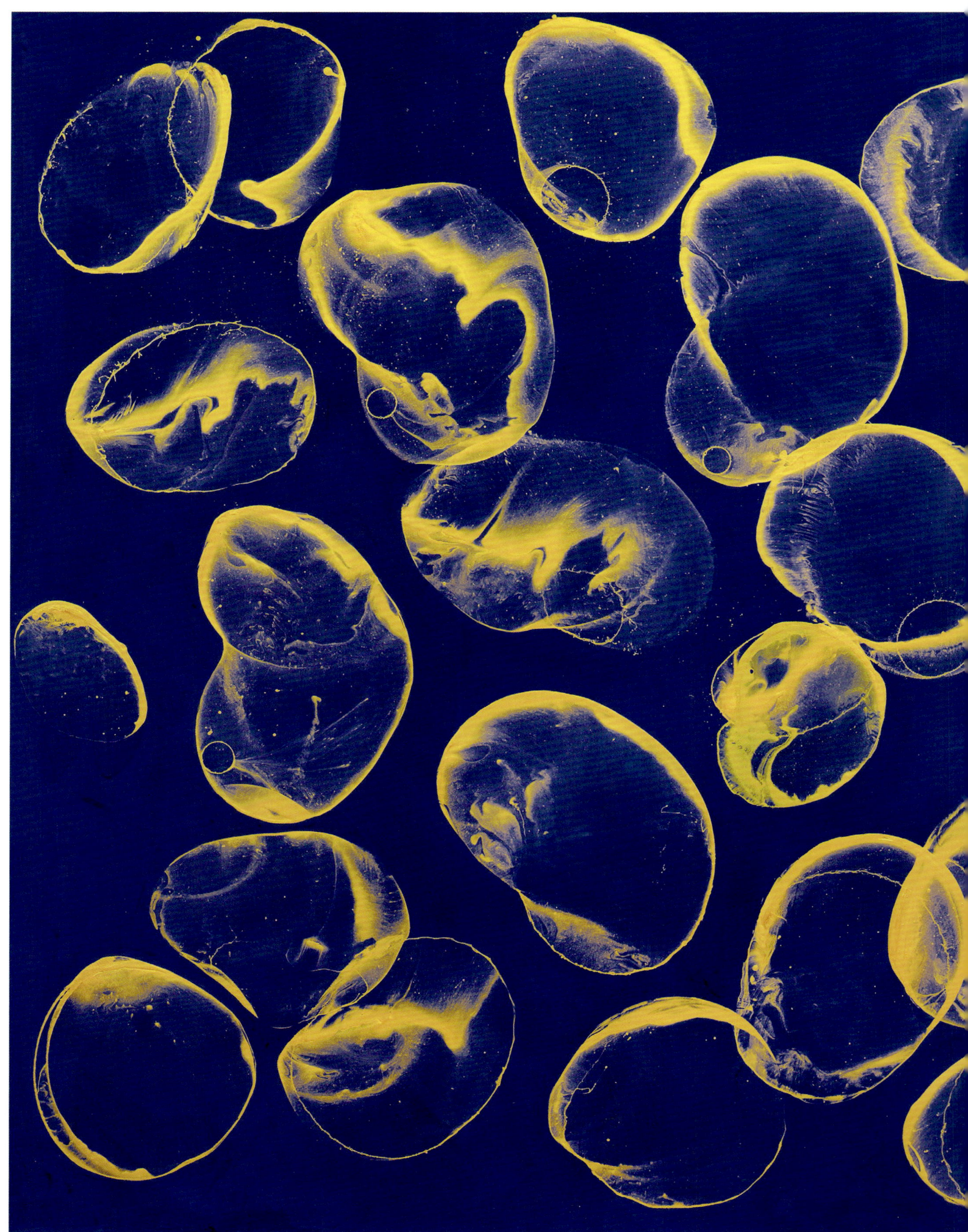

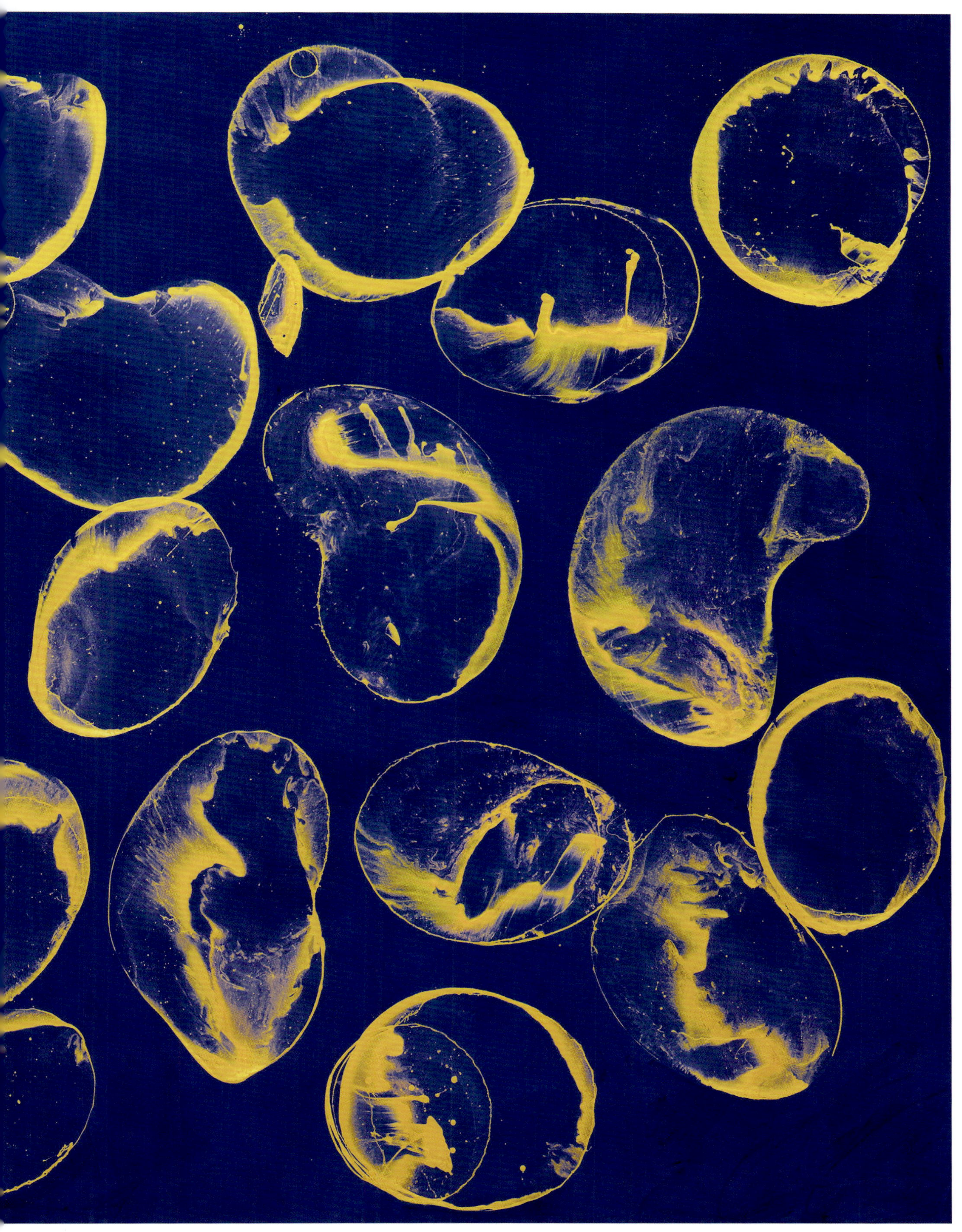

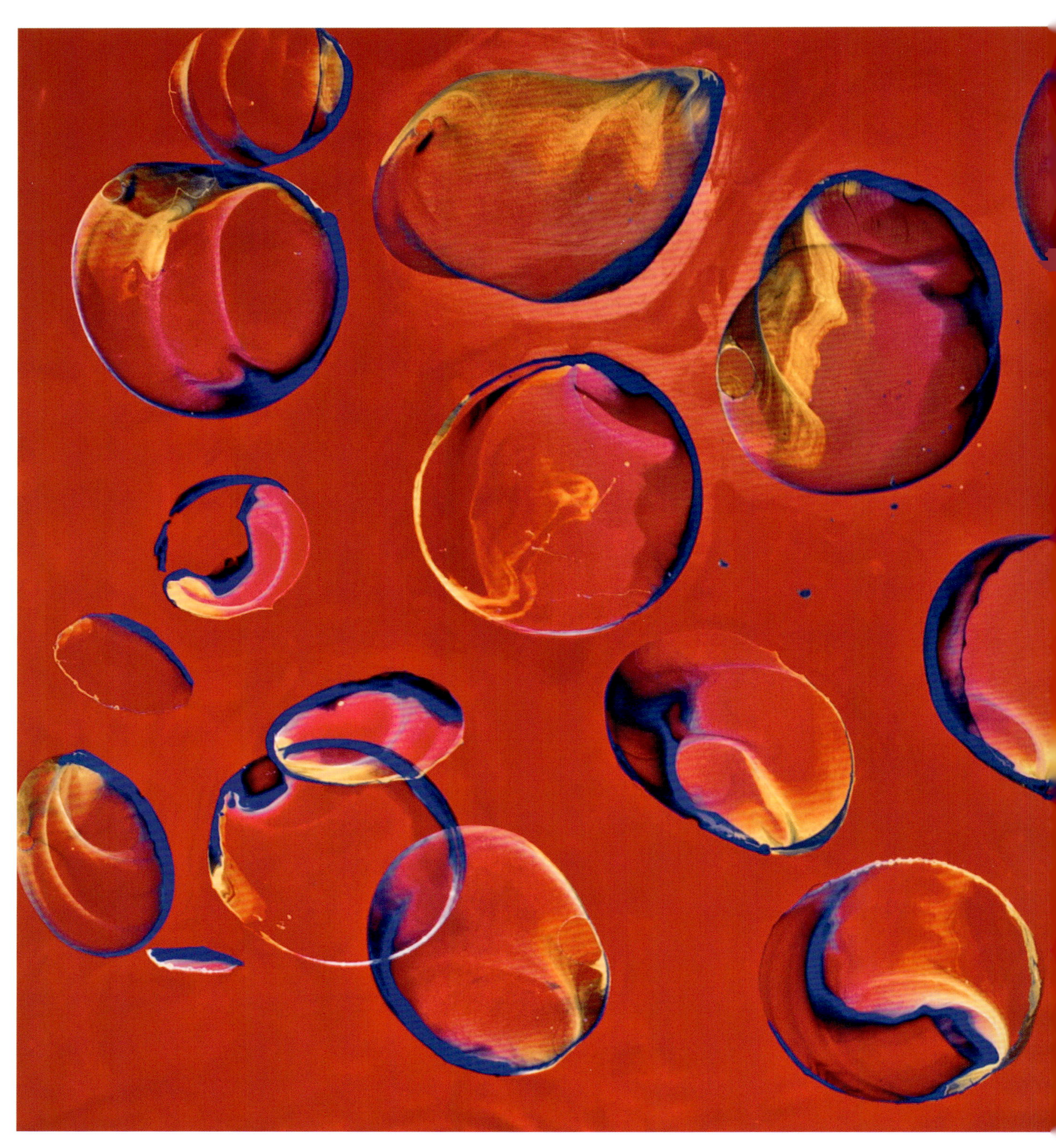

Rohayhu, 2024
Soap-lye and pigments on canvas
205 × 400 cm

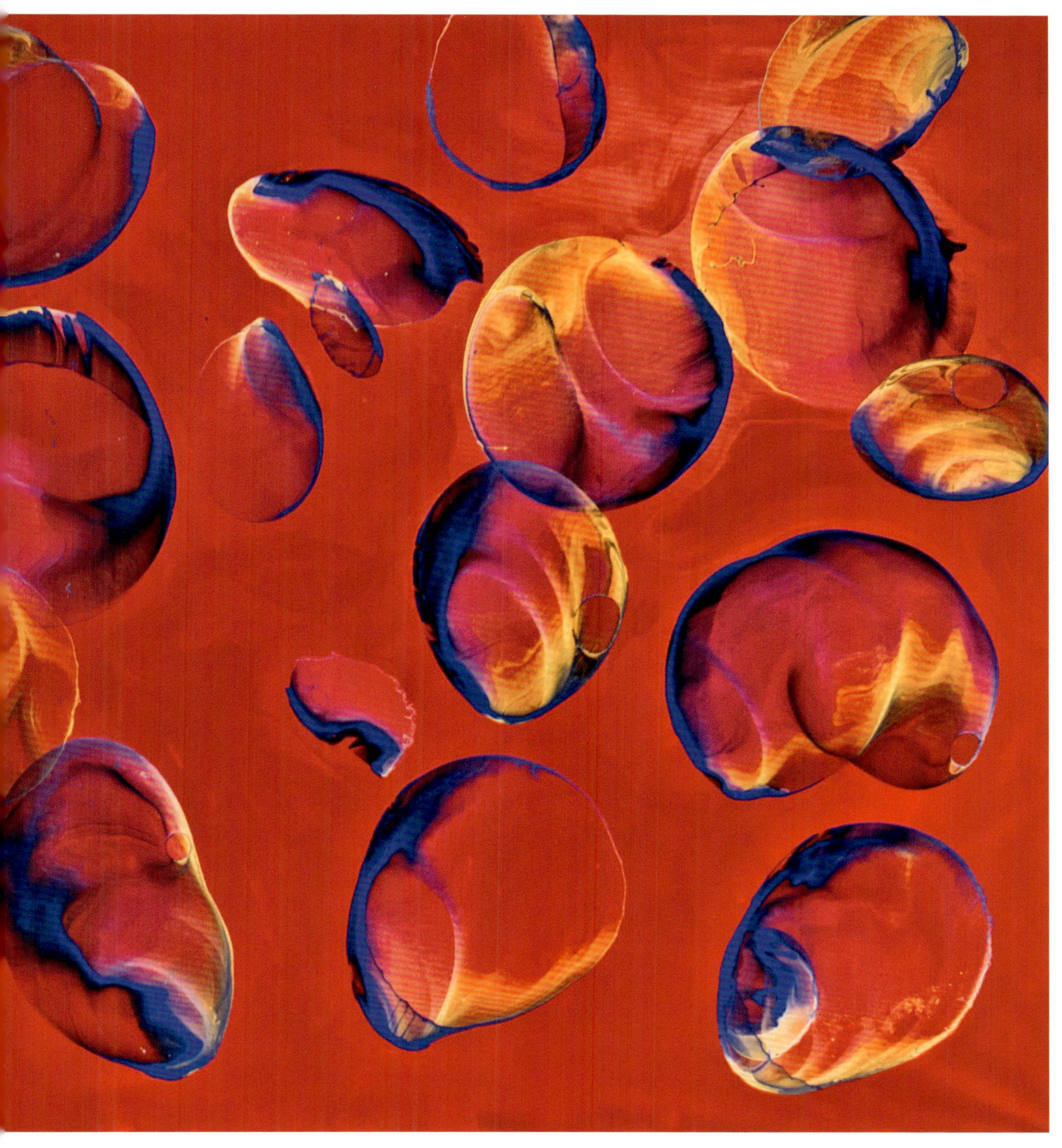

DURING THE MID-
EIGHTIES.
THE DOCTRINE OF
POST-MODERNISM
PREDOMINATED IN THE
ARTWORLD, WHICH
SAYS THAT
NOTHING NEW CAN
BE INVENTED. THIS
FORCED ME MORE AND
MORE TO CREATE
THE SOAPBUBBLE PAINTINGS

GS

WORKS OF ART
ARE LIVING,
BREATHING
BEINGS AND
THEY SLIGHTLY
VIBRATE

Yenni 2, 2023–24
Metal structure and glass
105 × 100 × 110 cm

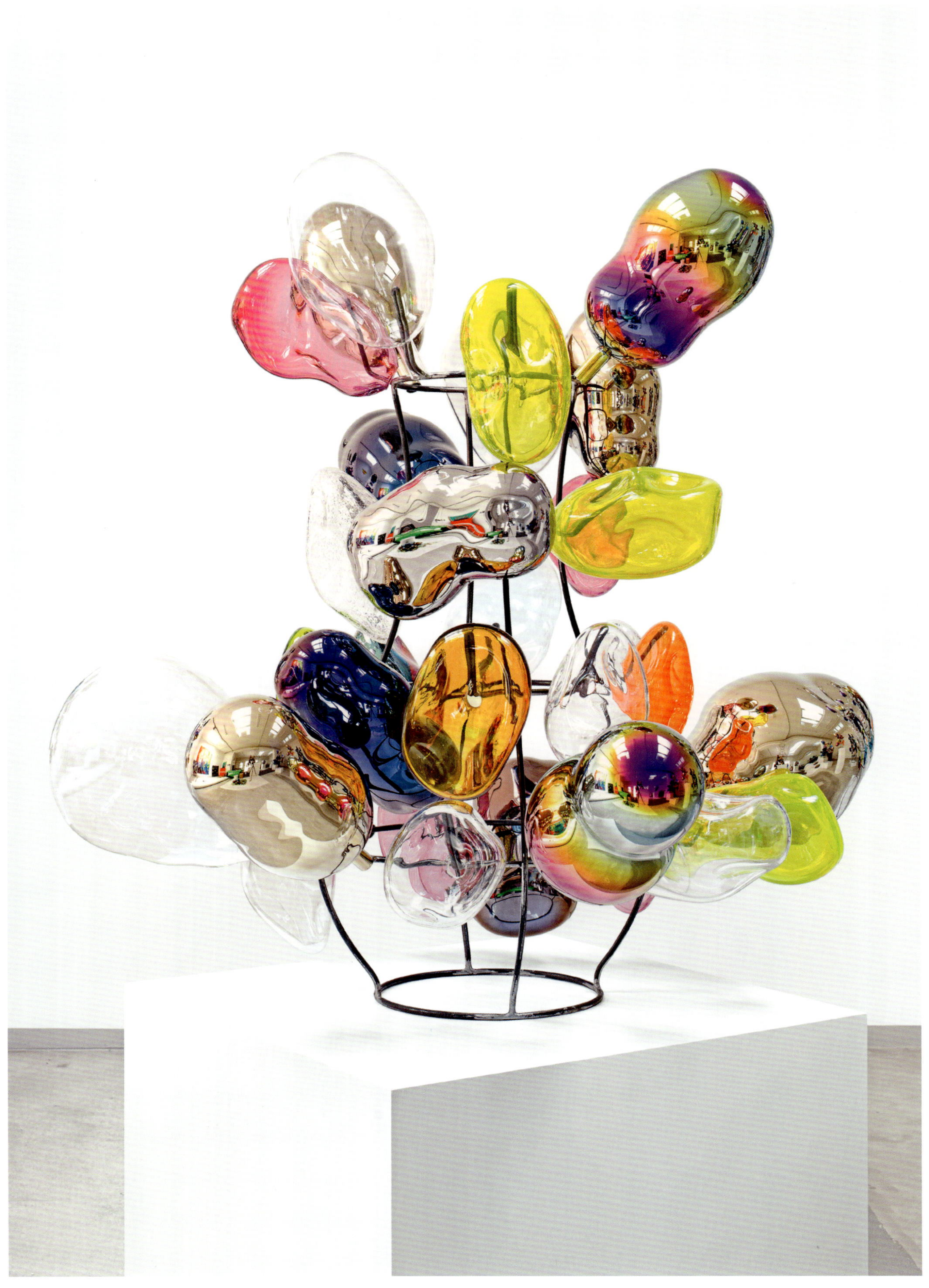

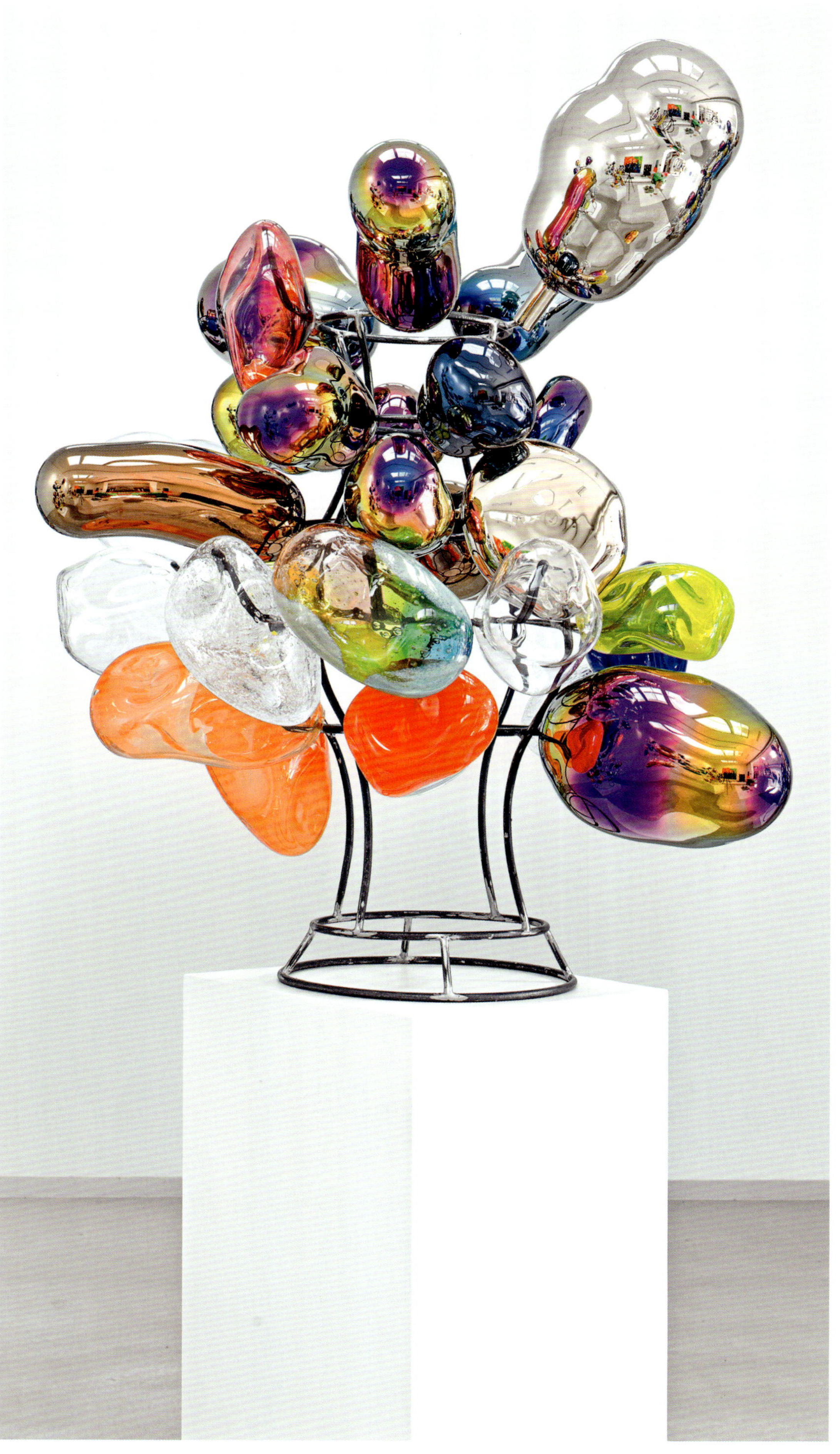

Yenni 3, 2023–24
Metal structure and glass
95 × 80 × 60 cm

Yenni 4, 2023–24
Metal structure and glass
170 × 130 × 110 cm

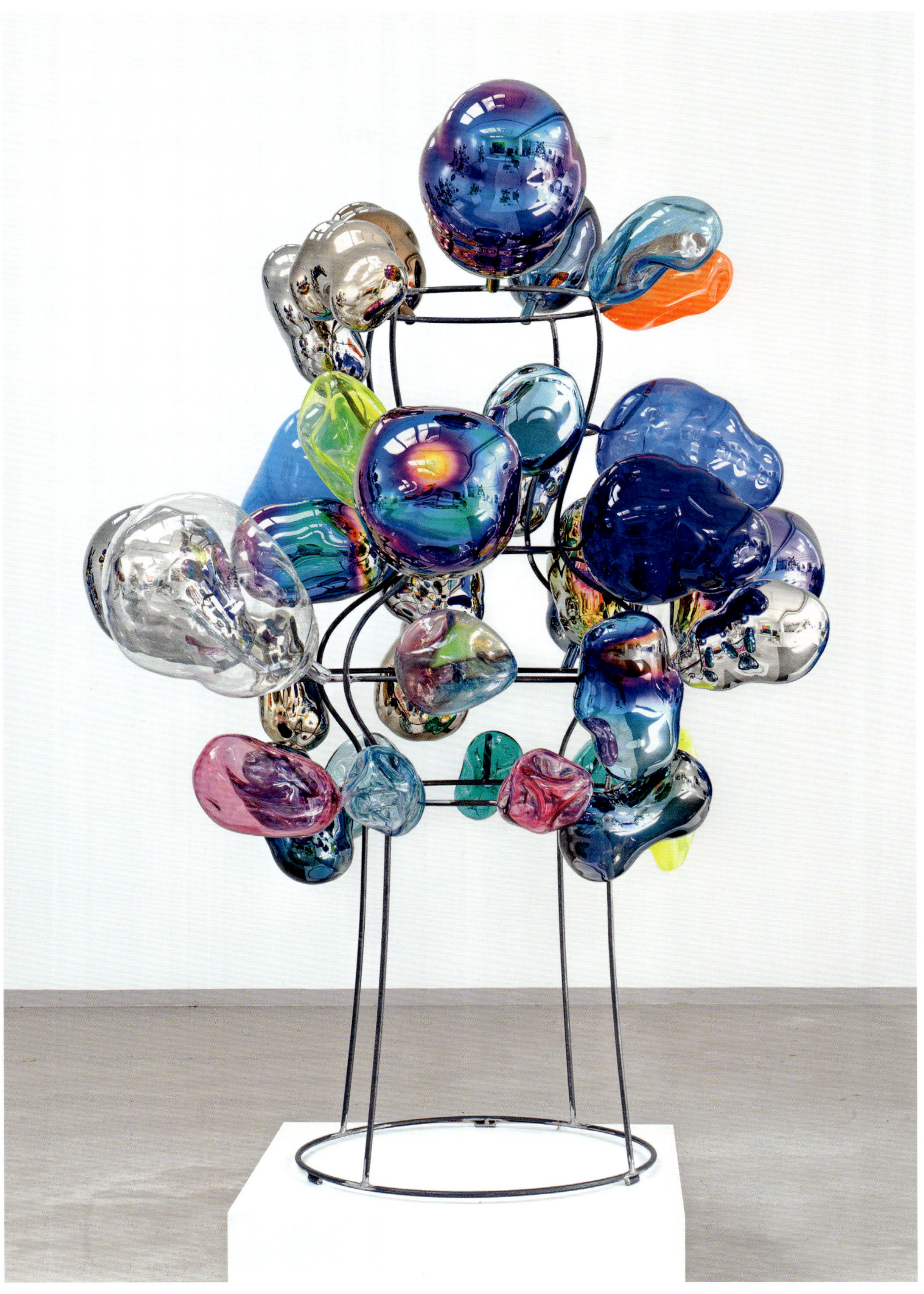

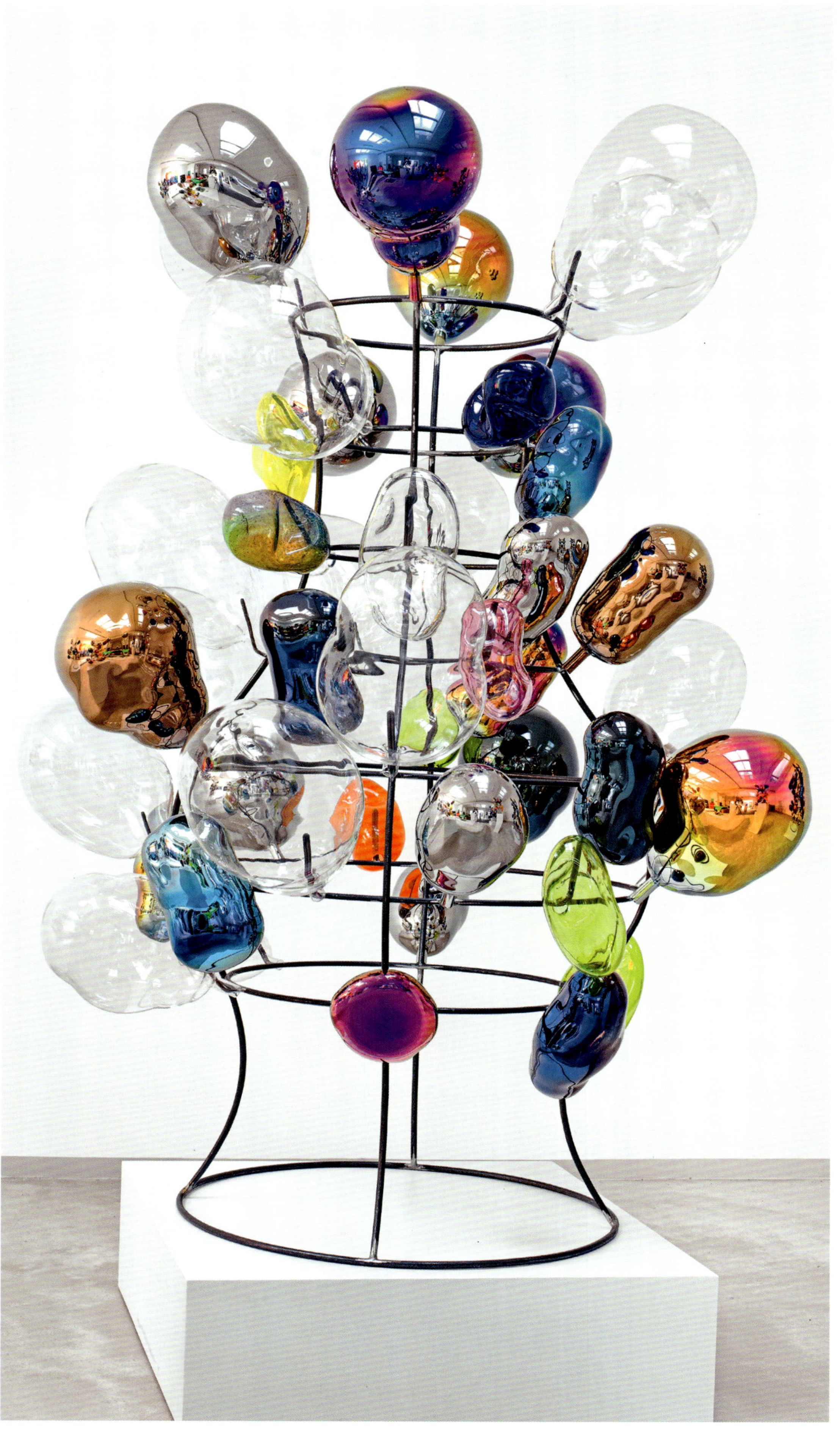

Ruth 2, 2023–24
Metal structure and glass
190 × 140 × 140 cm

Ruth 3, 2023–24
Metal structure and glass
200 × 135 × 135 cm

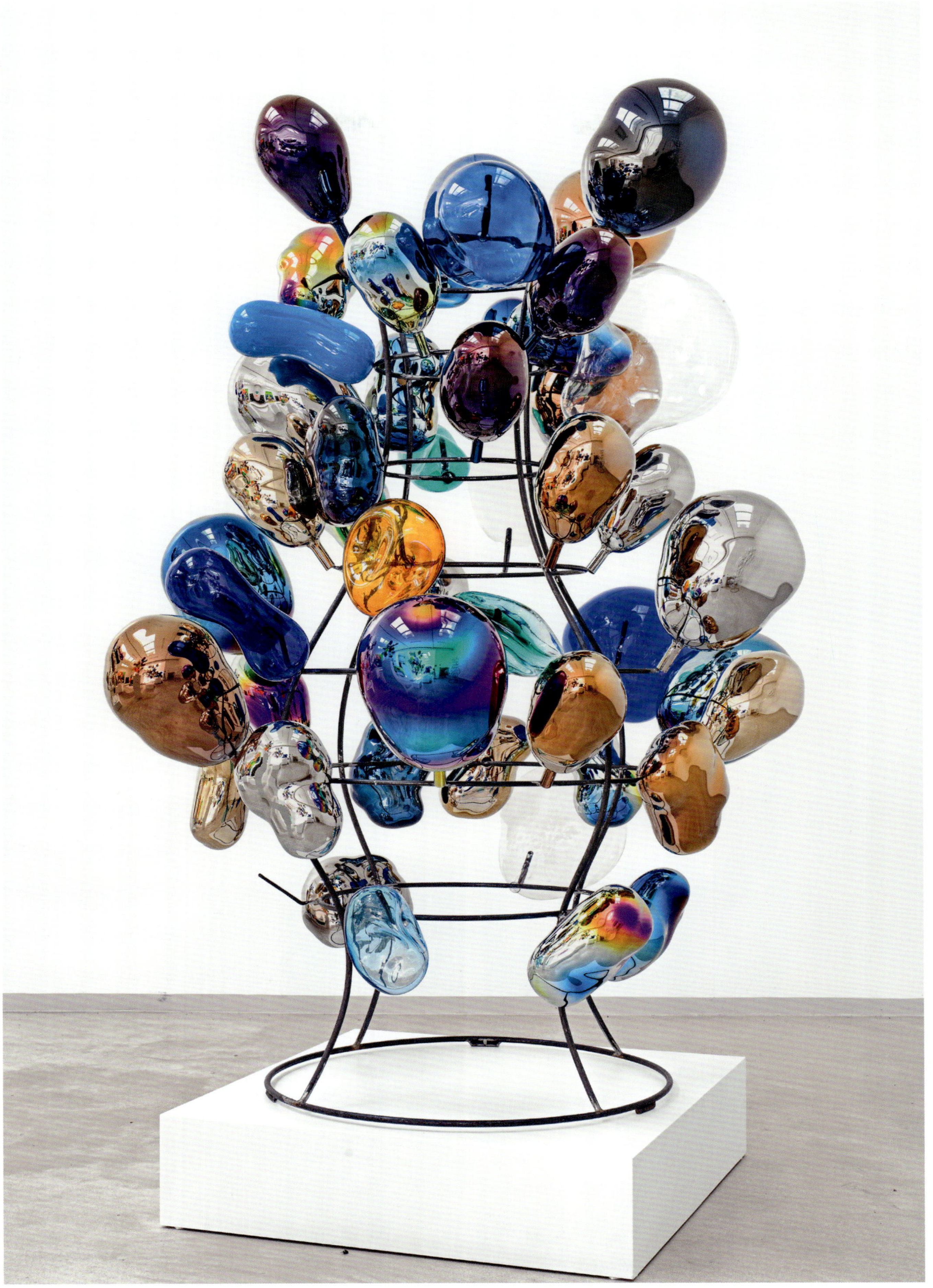

Ruth 4, 2023–24
Metal structure and glass
80 × 80 × 80 cm

Ruth 5, 2023–24
Metal structure and glass
175 × 120 × 130 cm

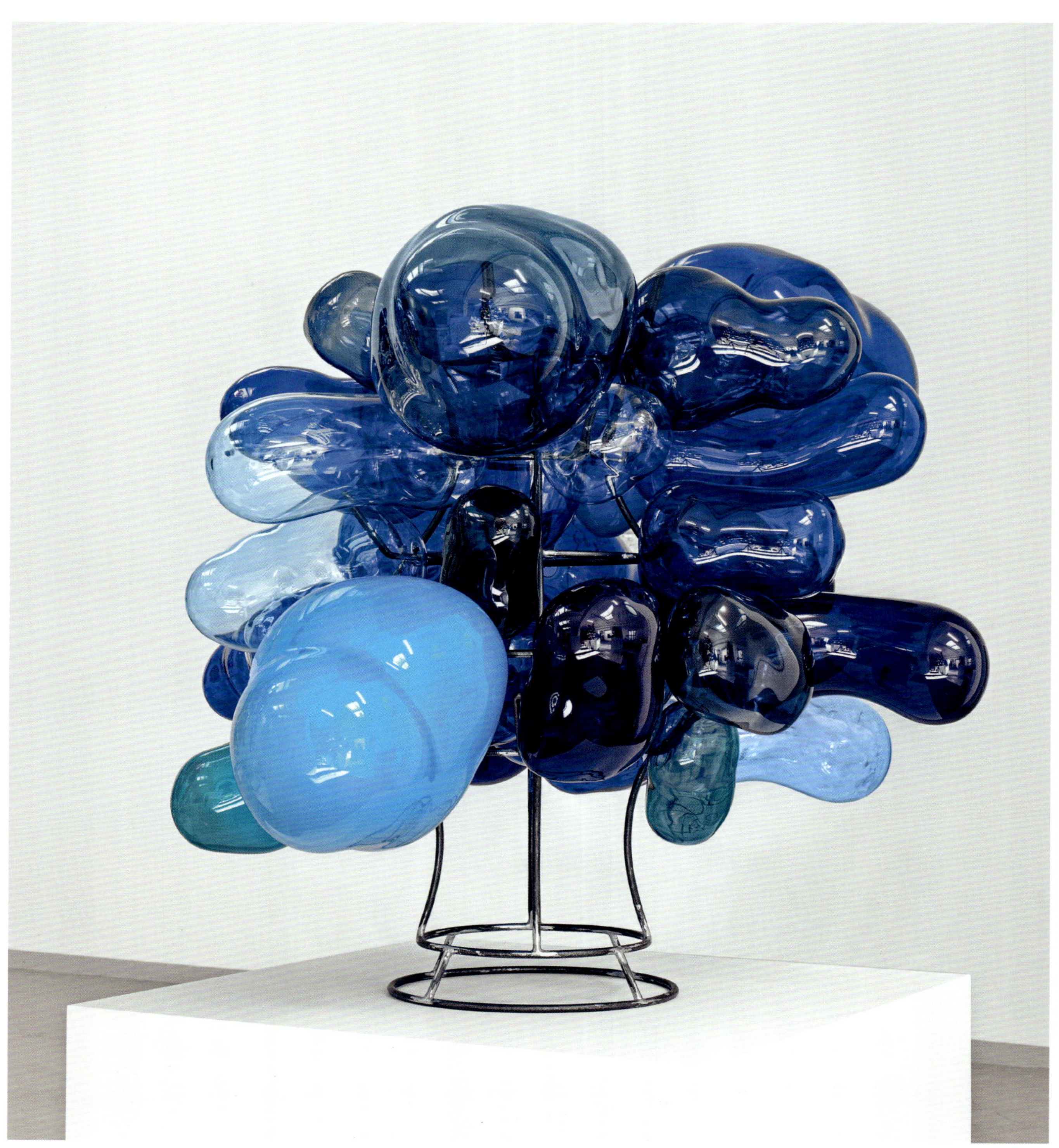

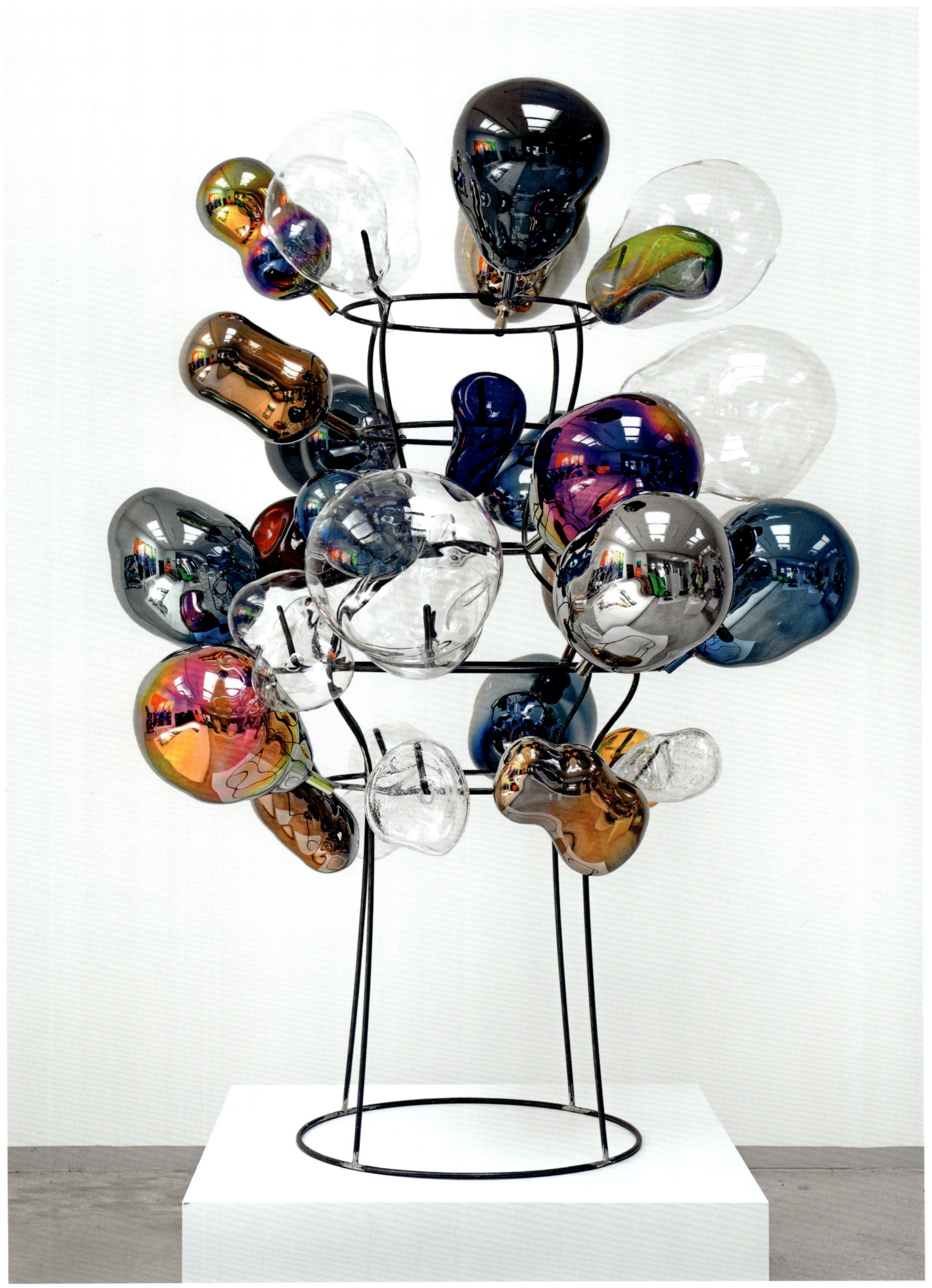

Open Bubbles Condensation
Cube, 2024
Acrylic glass box, glass,
condensed water
76 × 76 × 76 cm

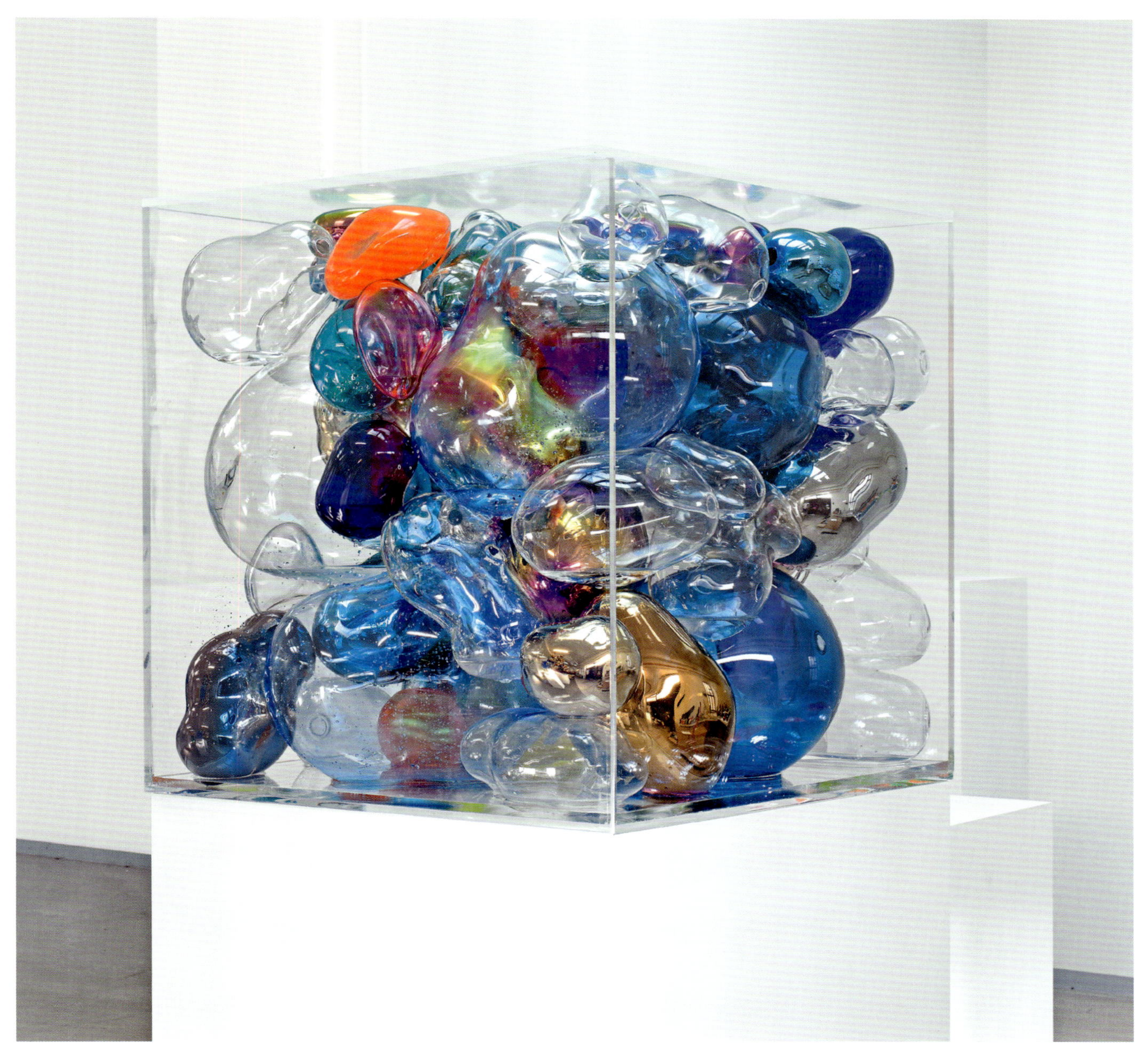

THE LIFE OF THE
SOAP BUBBLE
LASTS EIGHT
SECONDS.

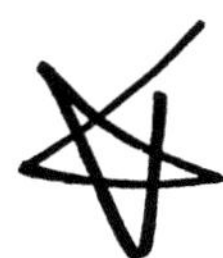

EVERY BUBBLE PAINTING
IS A REHEARSAL —
IT CAN NEVER
BE REPEATED.

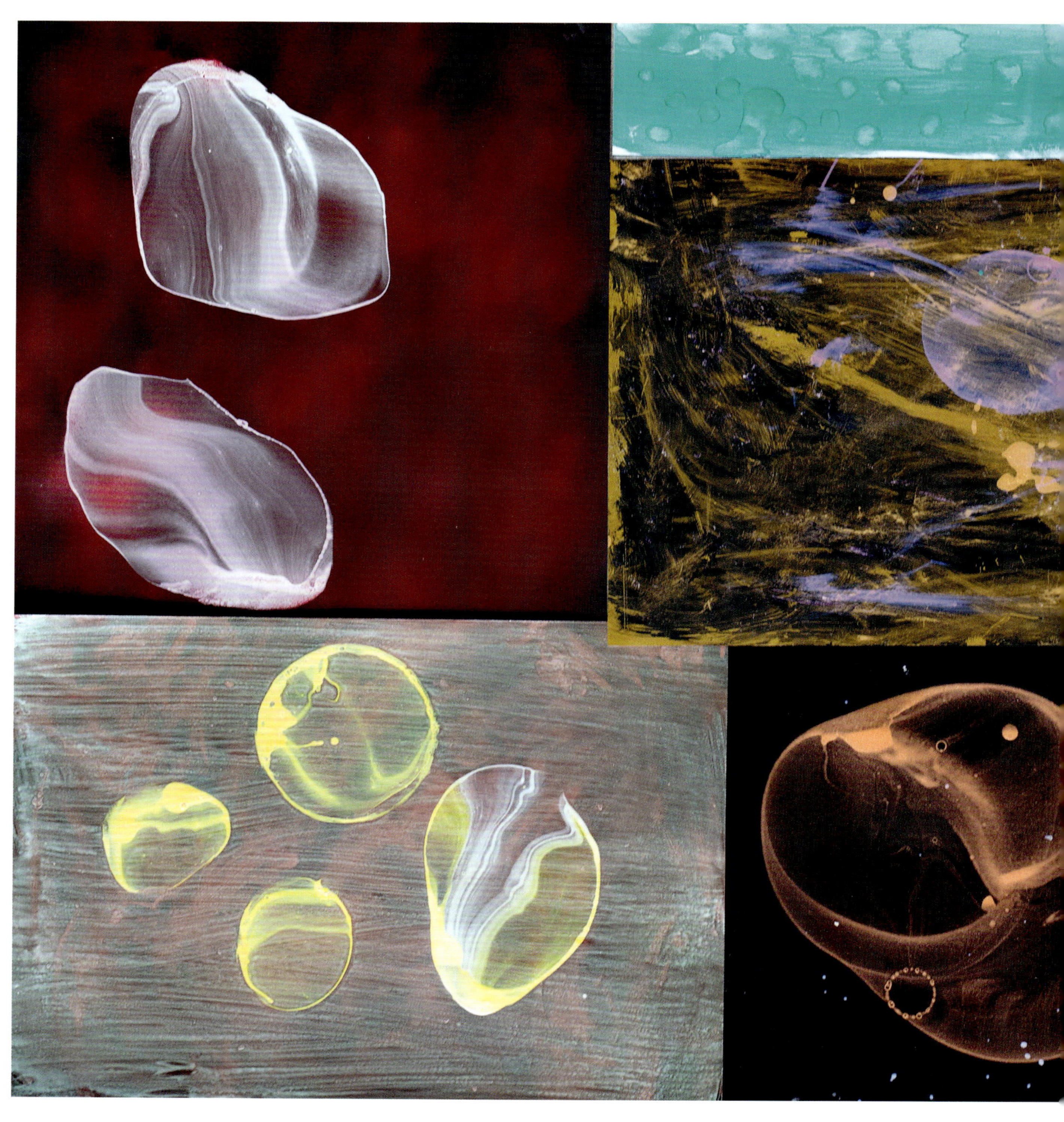

Odpad 1 (Collage), 2023–24
Soap-lye and pigments on paper
90 × 180 cm

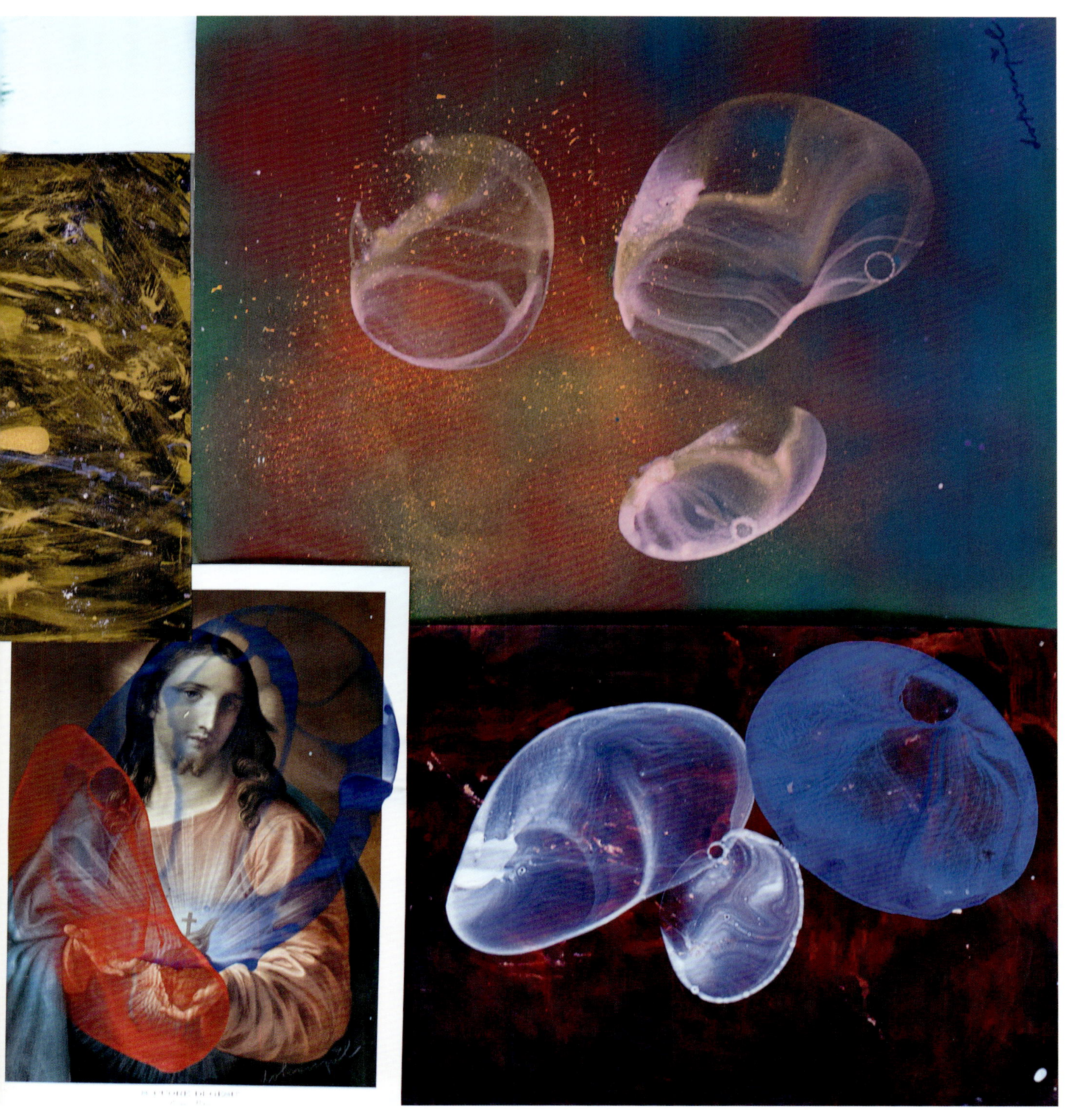

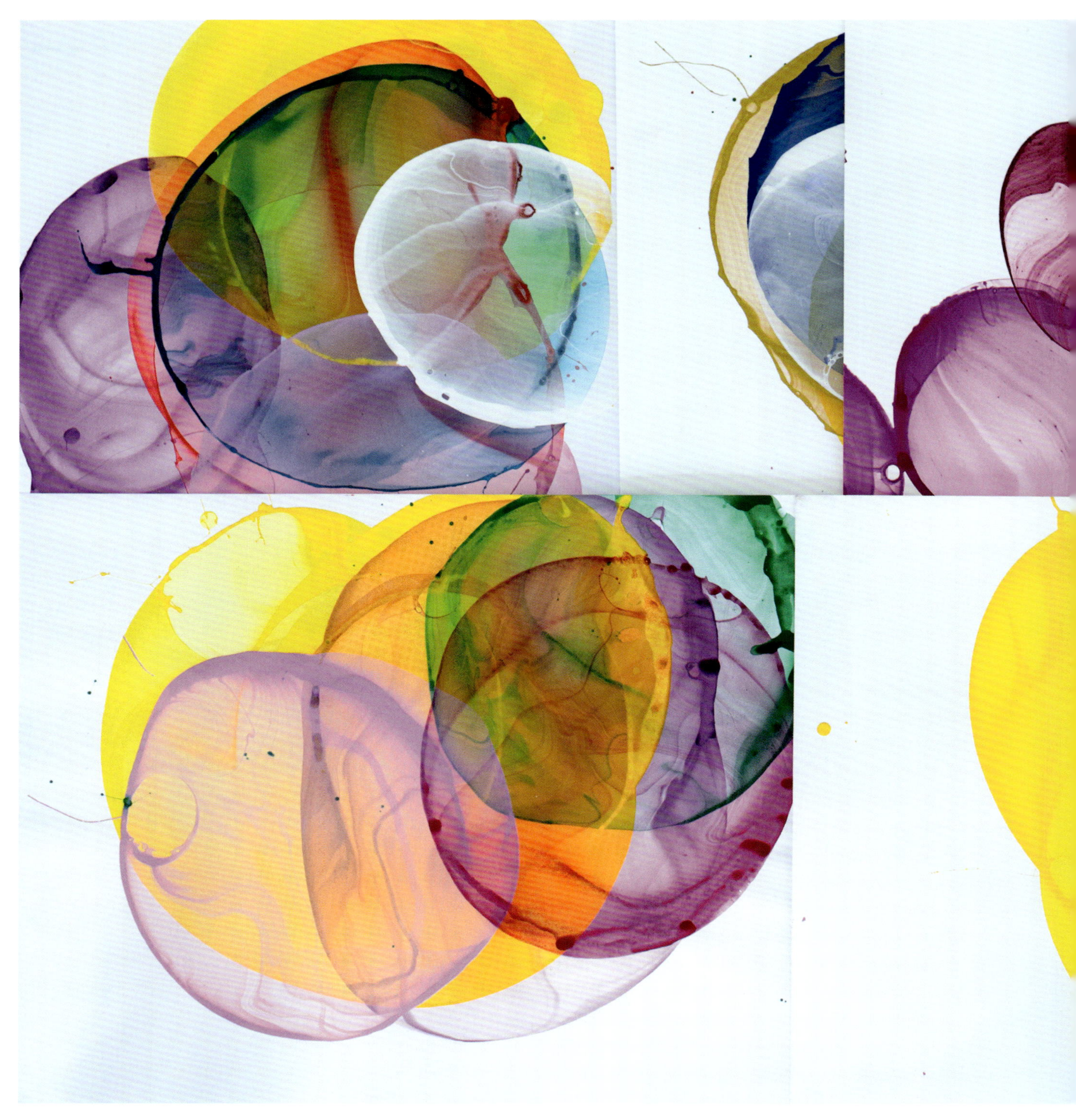

Odpad 2 (Collage), 2023–24
Soap-lye and pigments on paper
90 × 180 cm

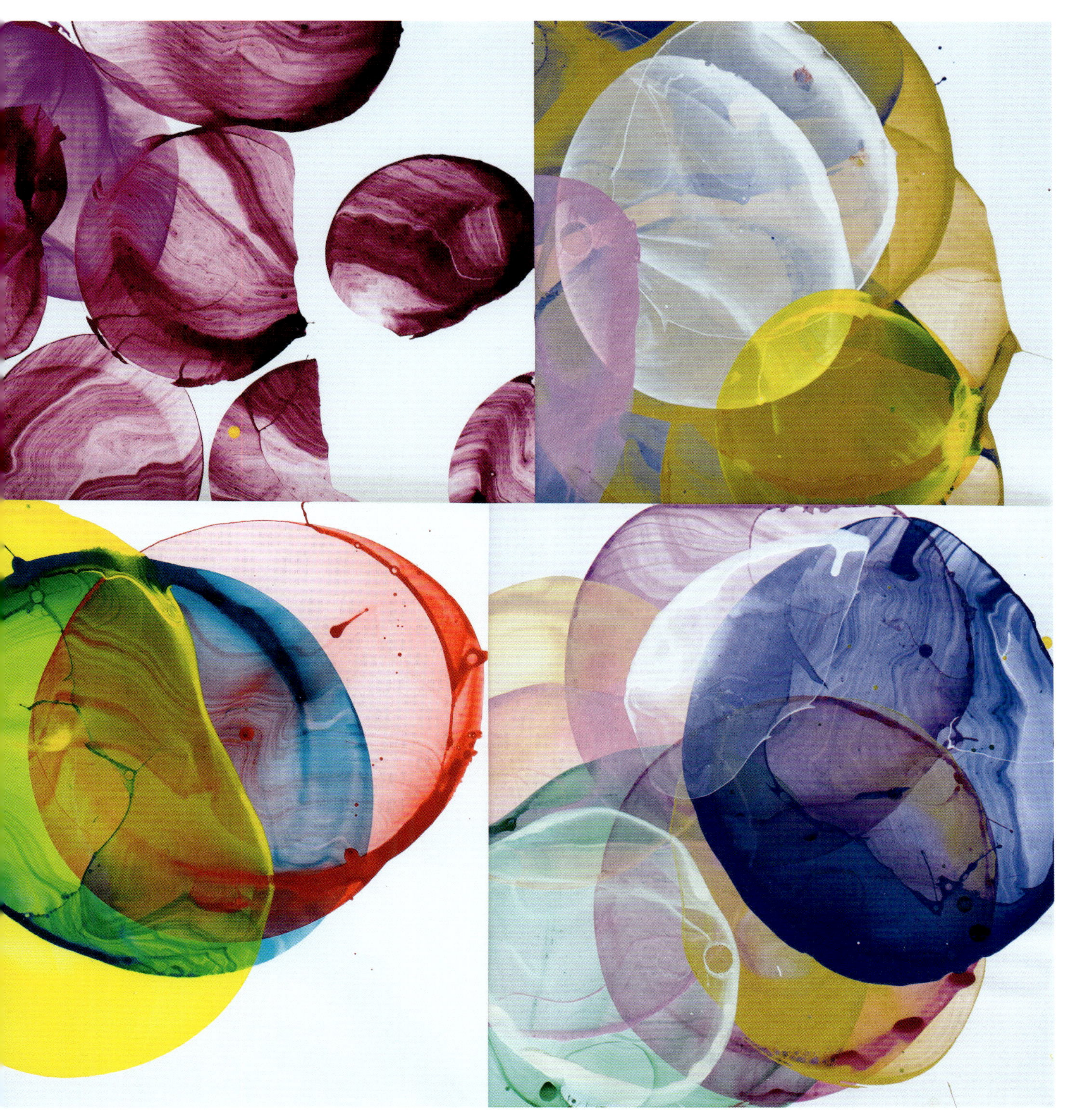

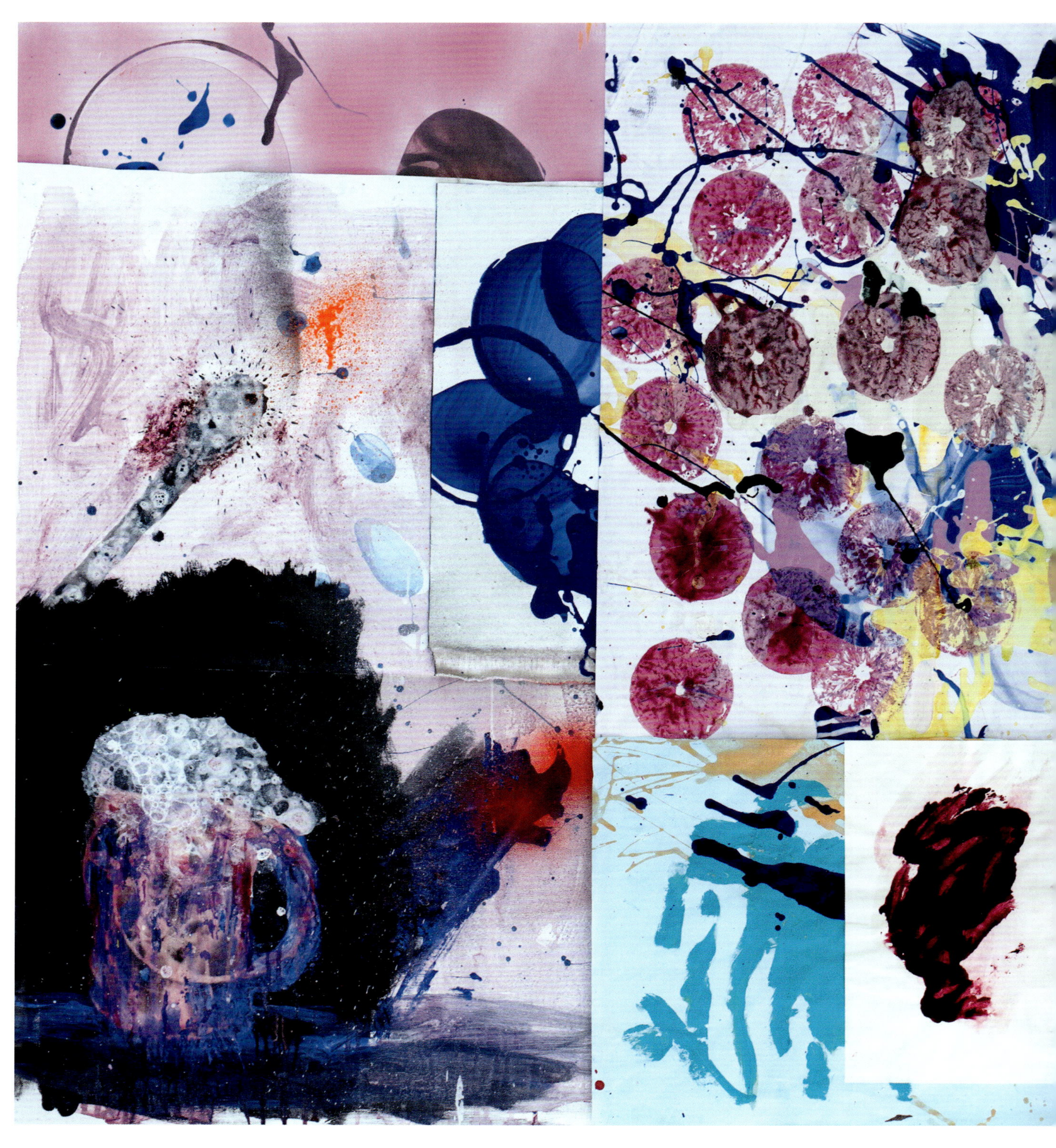

Odpad 3 (Collage), 2023–24
Soap-lye and pigments on paper
90 × 180 cm

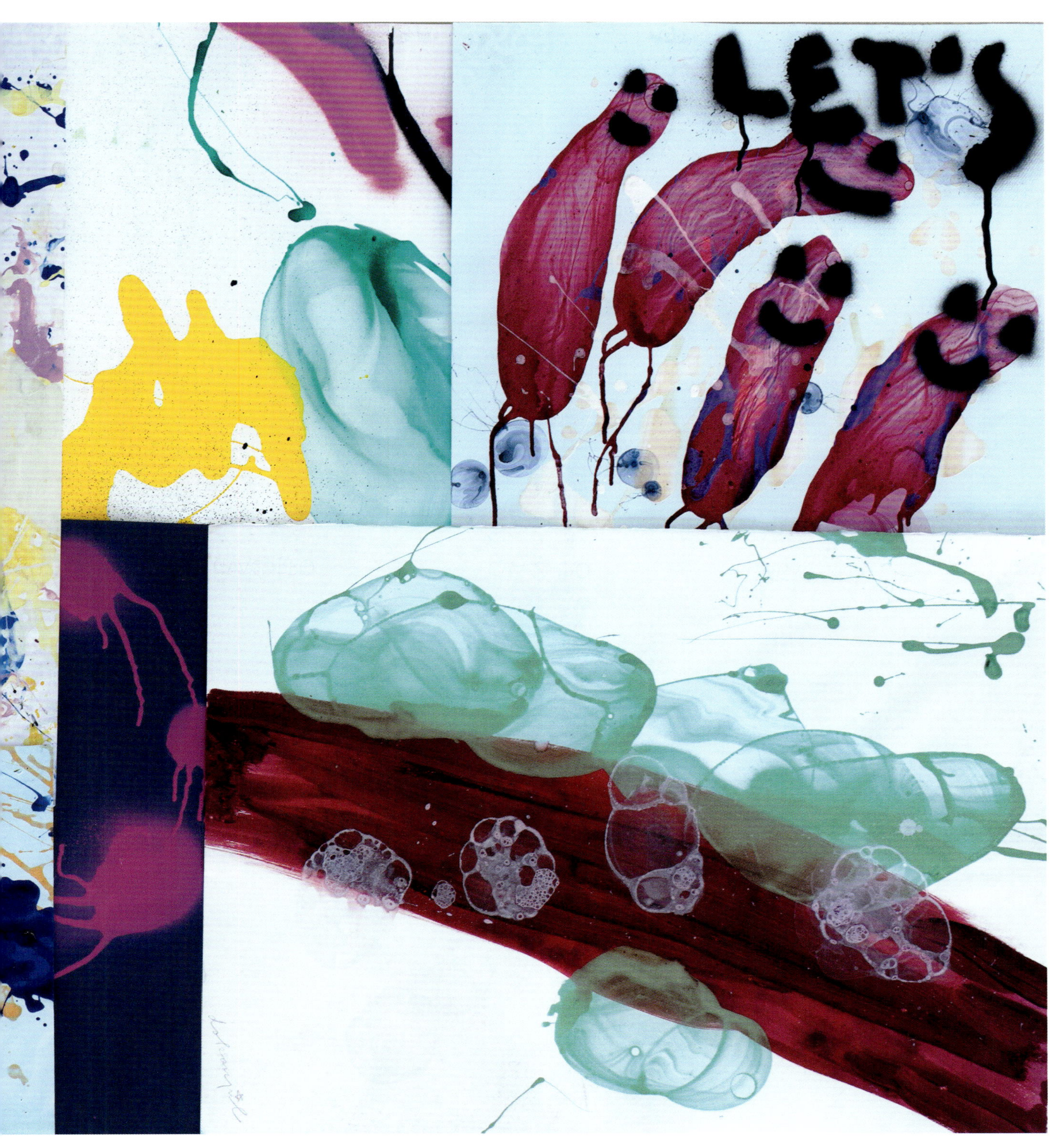
LET'S

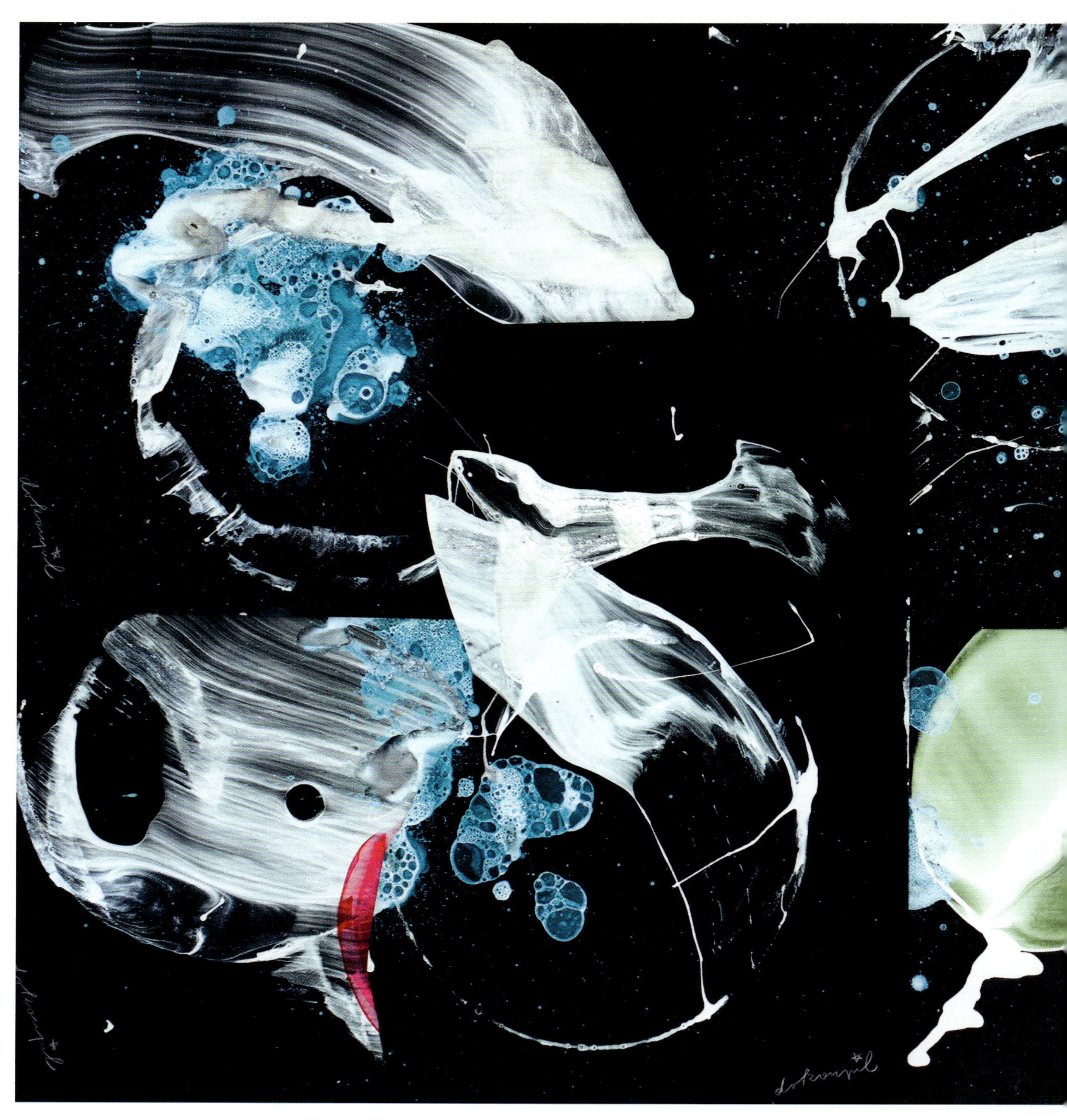

Odpad 4 (Collage), 2023–24
Soap-lye and pigments on paper
90 × 180 cm

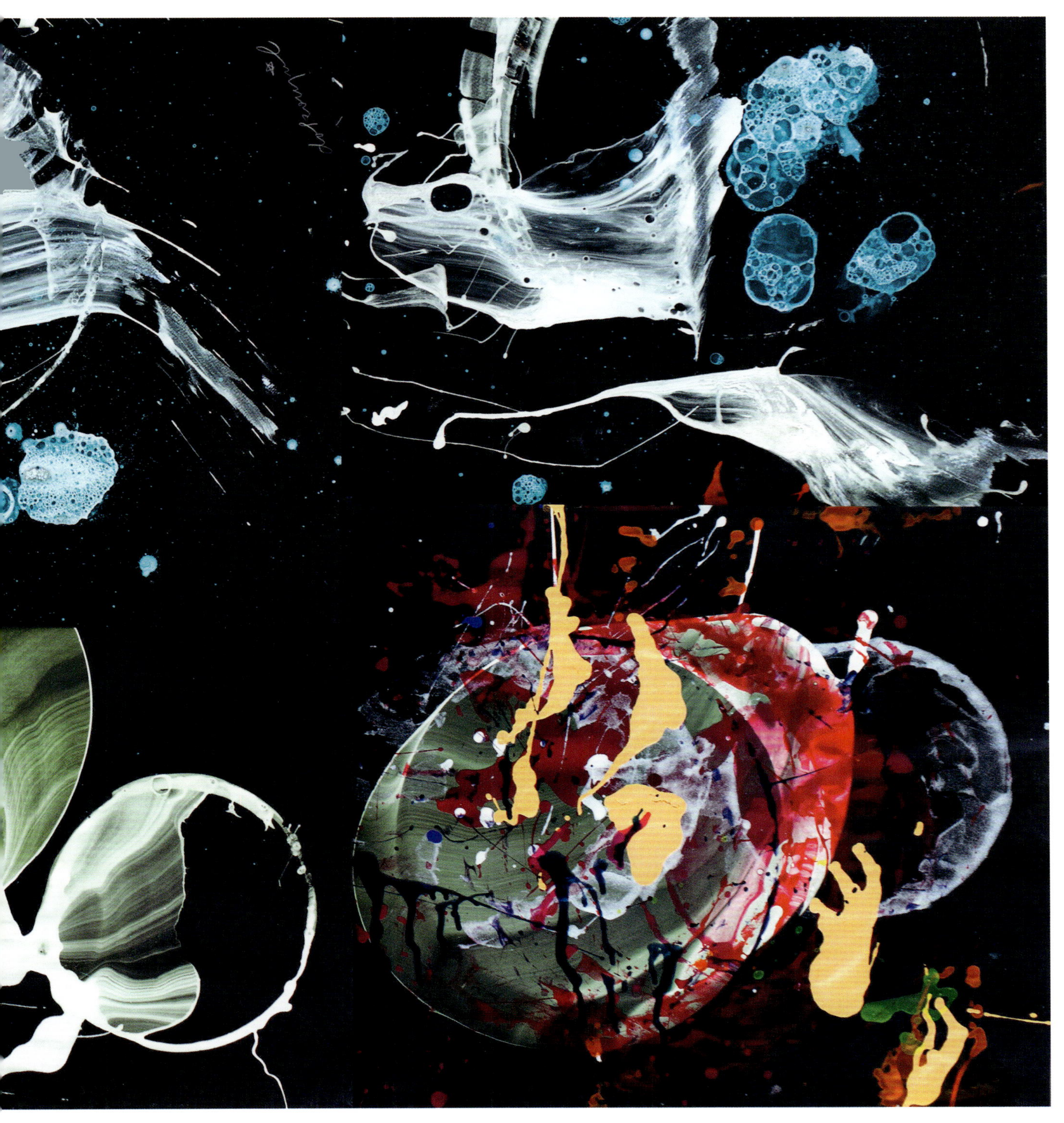

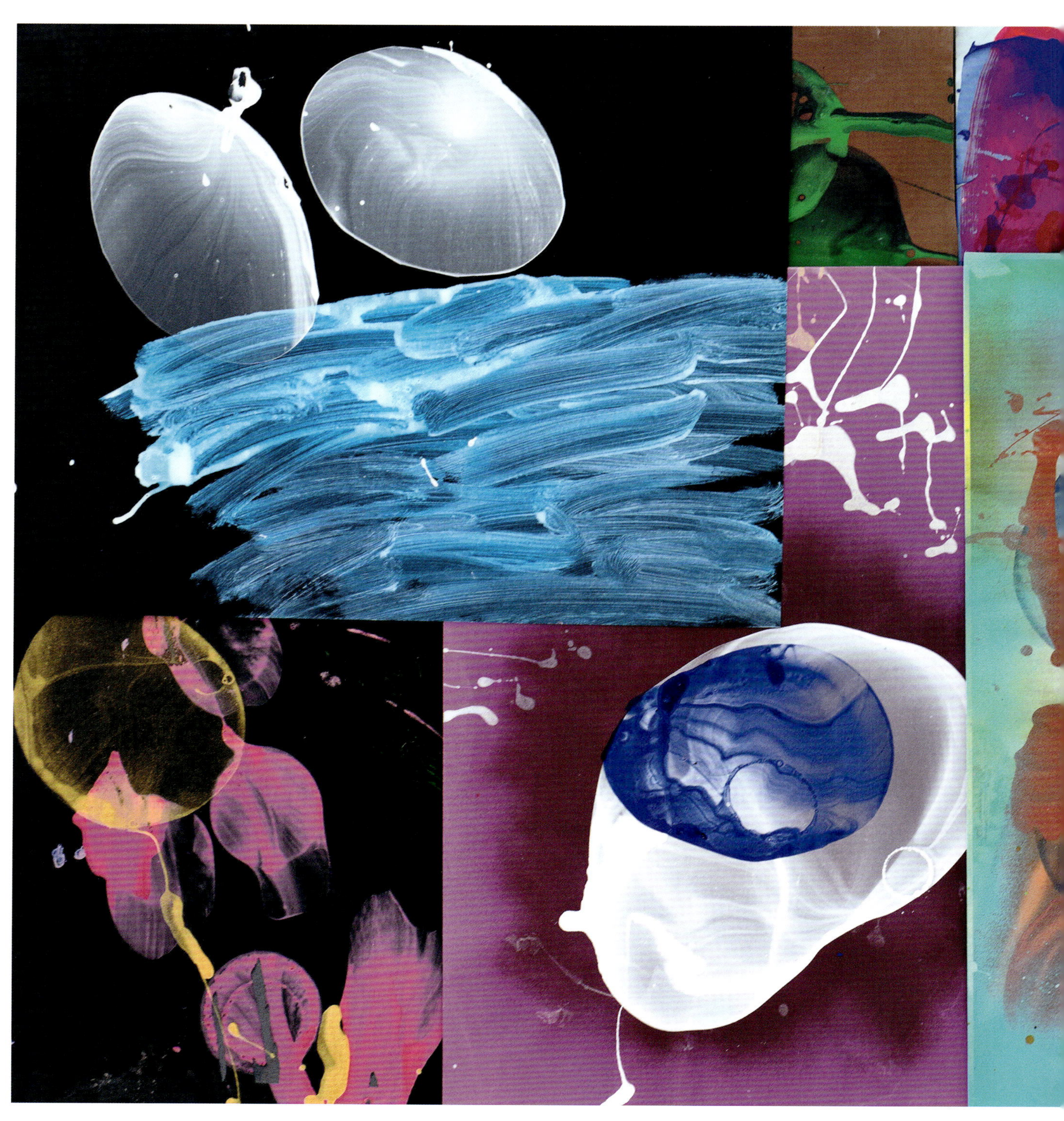

Odpad 5 (Collage), 2023–24
Soap-lye and pigments on paper
90 × 180 cm

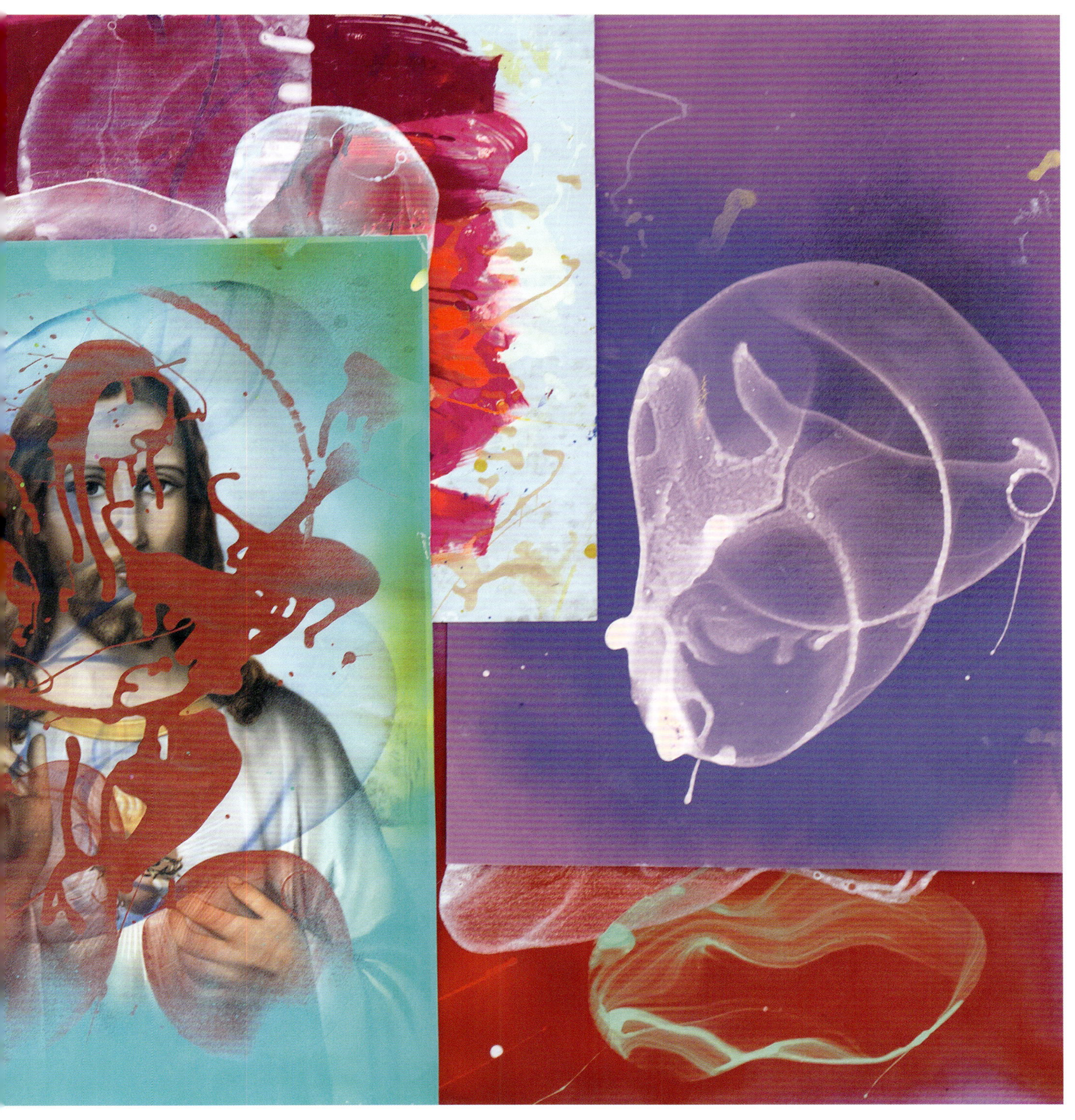

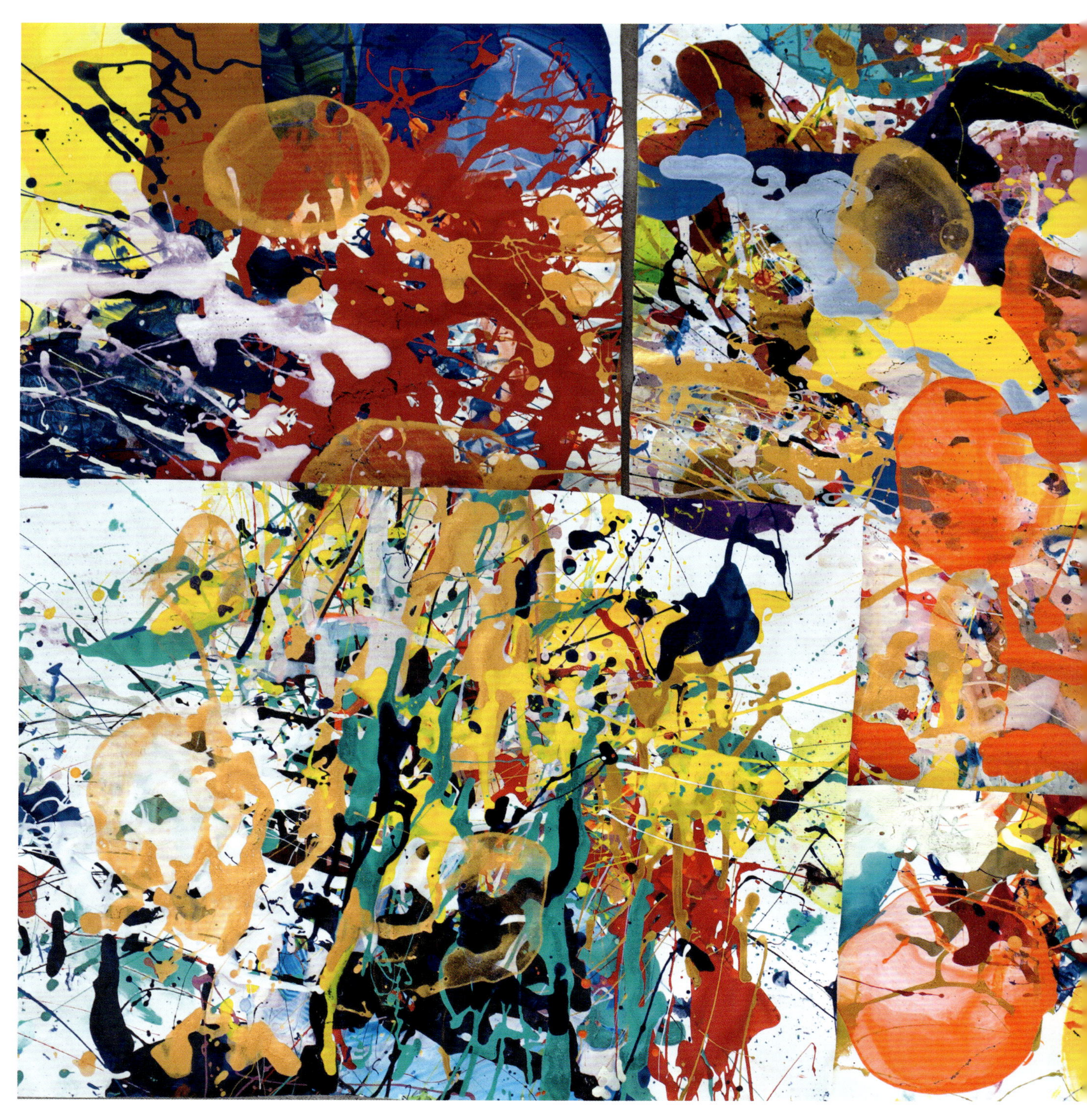

Odpad 6 (Collage), 2023–24
Soap-lye and pigments on paper
90 × 180 cm

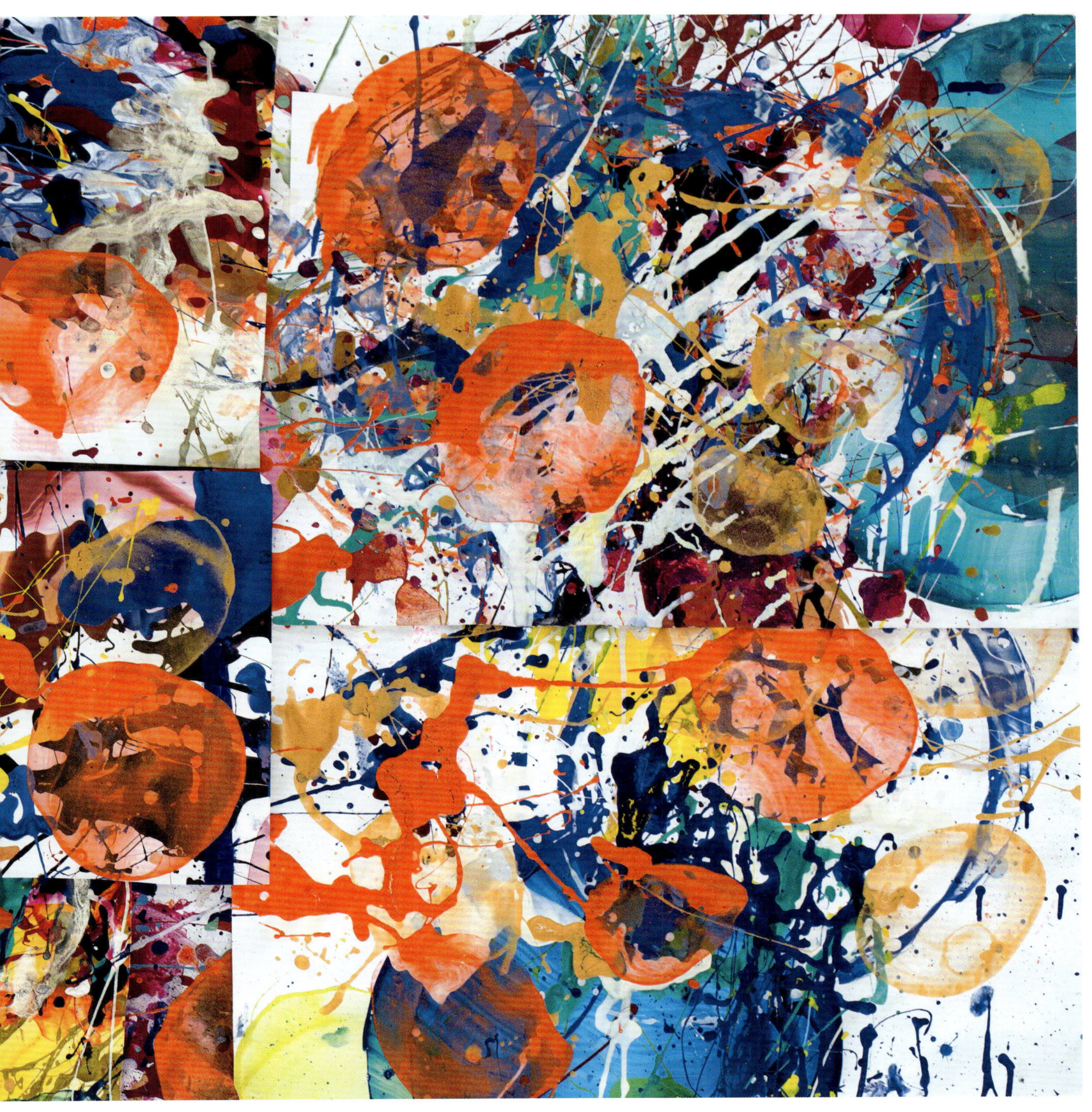

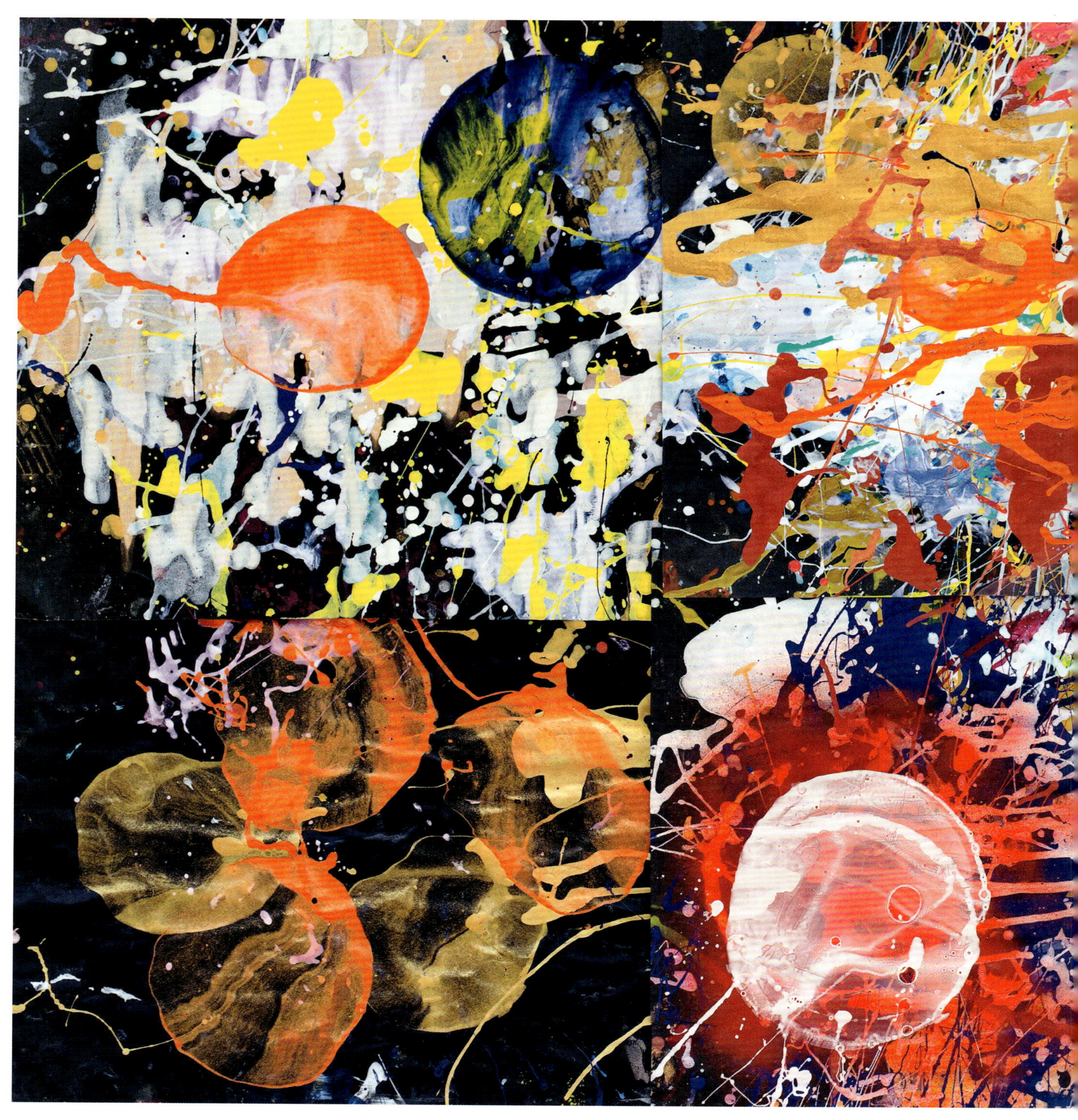

Odpad 7 (Collage), 2023–24
Soap-lye and pigments on paper
90 × 180 cm

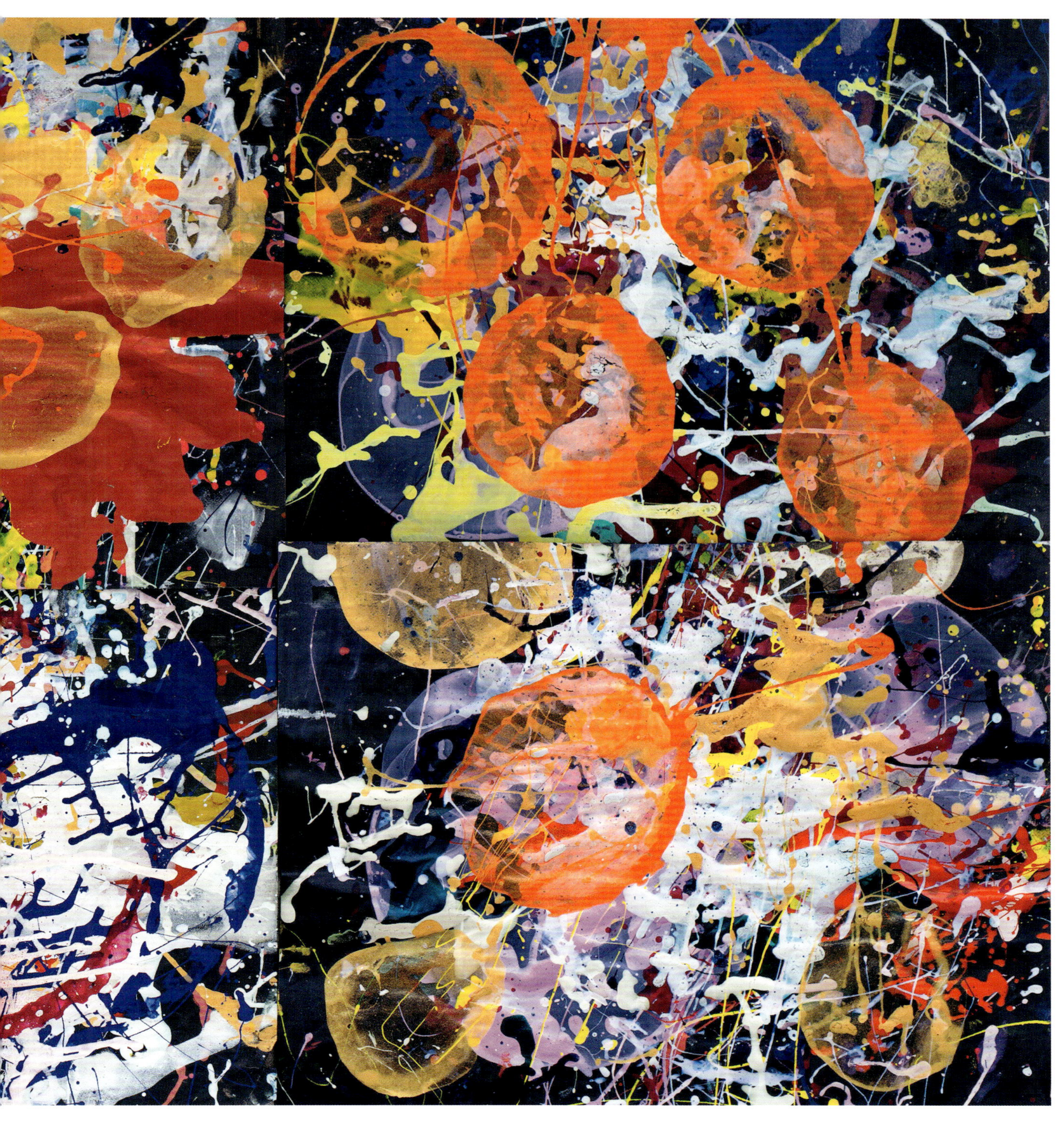

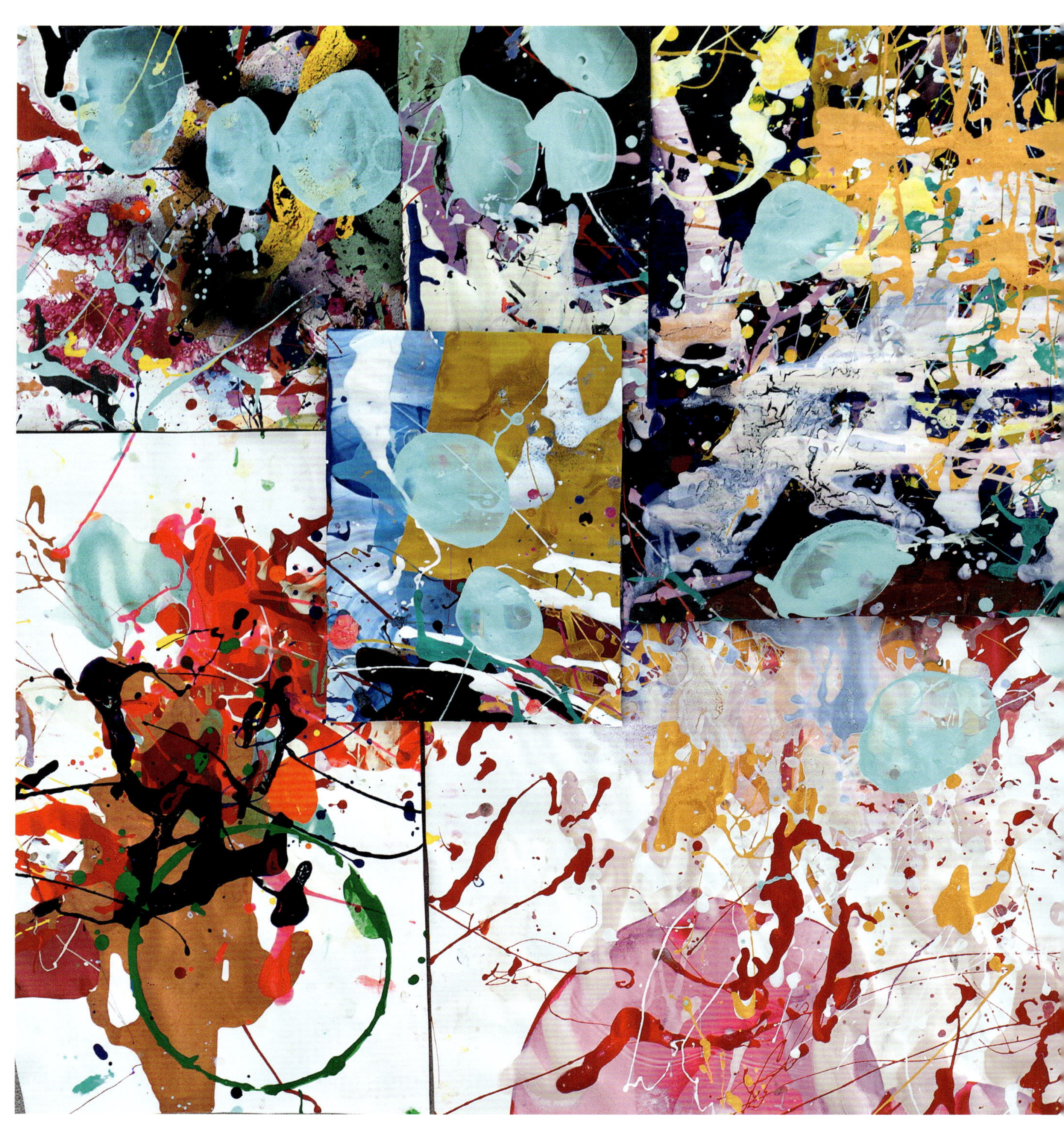

Odpad 8 (Collage), 2023–24
Soap-lye and pigments on paper
90 × 180 cm

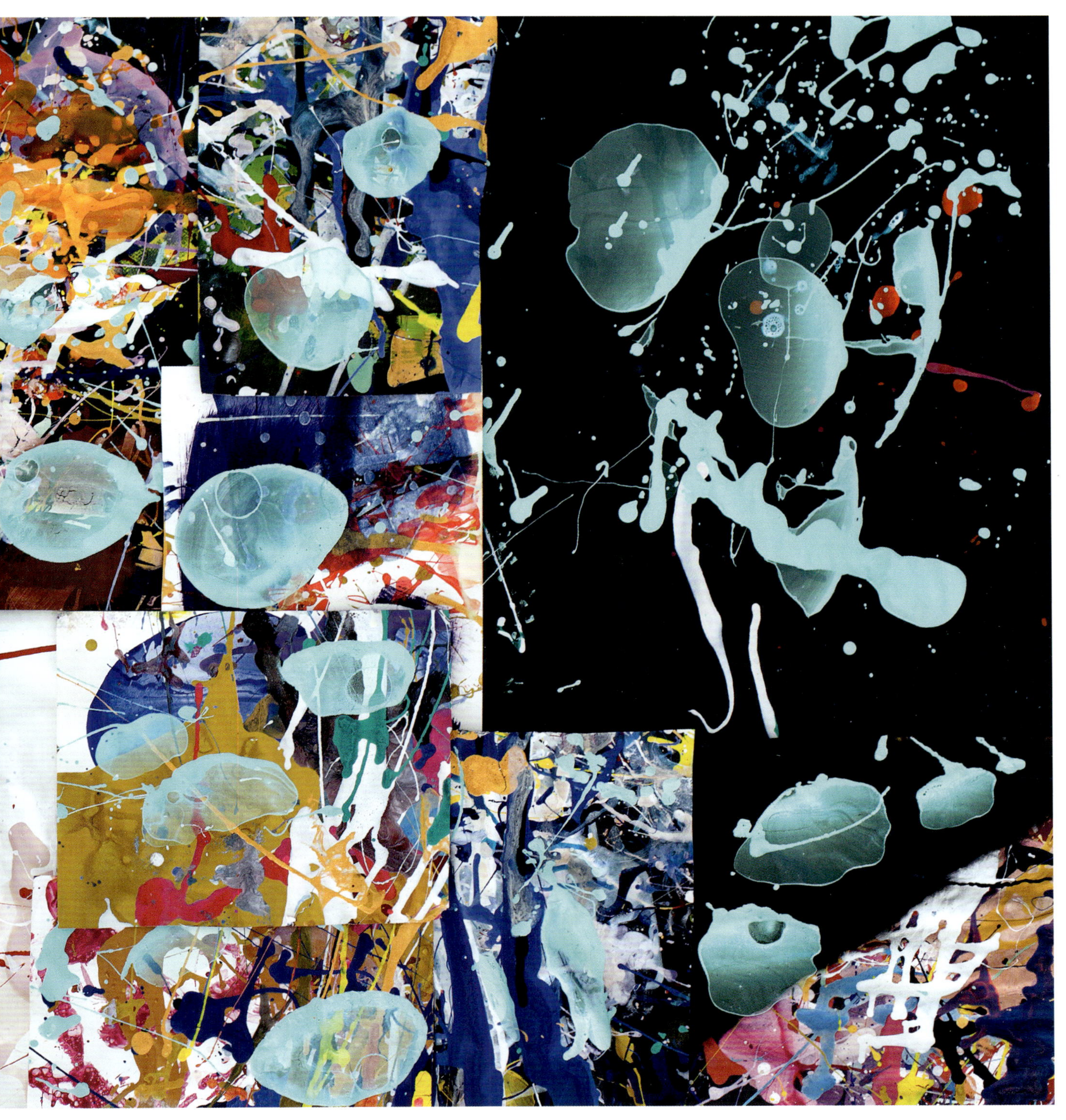

AS A   CHILD

I MADE BUBBLES

WITH THE STEM

OF   A DANDELI-
ON
PLANT.....'
IT GAVE ME A
STRANGE BITTER
TASTE.

BUBBLES ARE
LIKE LITTLE CHILDREN.
YOU CANNOT LEAVE
THEM ALONE FOR
ONE SECOND AND
THEY ALWAYS
NEED TENDER CARE.

Biographies

JIRI GEORG DOKOUPIL

Jiri Georg Dokoupil's main subject is painting. He refuses to be subordinated to a personal style, attitude or conventional artistic approach. Instead, he operates in a free and not assignable manner right from the beginning of his career in the 1980s. The artist's open and experimental spirit creates a wide range of visual worlds through unconventional technical inventions: he puts color on canvas with a whip or with car tires, he creates candle paintings using soot or bound oil paints into soap bubbles, only to have them burst on his canvases. The artist is fixing the ephemeral within his pictorial inventions. Dokoupil's oeuvre today contains over 60 series and far more than 100 devised techniques or styles.

Biography

Jiri Georg Dokoupil was born in Krnov, former Czechoslovakia, in 1954. After the invasion of the Soviet army in Prague in 1968, he fled with his family to Germany.

From 1976 to 1978, he studied fine arts in Cologne, Frankfurt am Main, and in New York at The Cooper Union with the conceptual artist Hans Haacke. He was the co-founder of the Mülheimer Freiheit group in Cologne, which was a significant part of the Neue Wilde movement in Europe and the USA in the late 1970s and early 1980s. The group was associated with the legendary art dealer Paul Maenz who organized Dokoupil's first solo exhibition in Cologne in 1982. In their shared studio in Cologne on a street named Mülheimer Freiheit, the Neue Wilde sought to explore a contemporary expression for their art by using a neo-expressive, figurative style of intensely colorful painting with traditional subjects and by overriding the intellectual, reduced formal language of Minimal and Conceptual art. Dokoupil also taught as a guest professor at the Academy of Fine Arts of Düsseldorf from 1983 to 1984 and in Madrid during 1989.

Dokoupil developed a less wild, rather unusual working method and soon found his own radical subjective way with individual considerations. With his "book painting" shown at Documenta 7 in Kassel in 1982, he widely attracted the attention of the art world. Since then – besides the early group exhibitions with the Mülheimer Freiheit – Dokoupil's work has been seen in numerous one-man shows in galleries, museums, and at other cultural sites worldwide.

Dokoupil lives and works between Berlin, Madrid, Prague, Rio de Janeiro, and Las Palmas.

Guest teaching semesters at the following art academies

Düsseldorf, Germany; Madrid, Spain; Amsterdam, The Netherlands; Santa Cruz de Tenerife, Spain; Kassel, Germany; Cuenca, Spain.

Selected one-man exhibitions

Osthaus Museum, Hagen (2021); Deichtorhallen, Hamburg (2005); Museu de Arte Moderna, São Paulo (2003); Palacio de Velázquez, Madrid (2000); Museum Moderner Kunst Stiftung Ludwig, Vienna (1997), Galerie Rudolfinum, Prague (1996); Museum Folkwang, Essen (1984); Kunstmuseum Luzern, Lucerne; Groninger Museum, Groningen; Espace Lyonnais d'Art Contemporain, Lyon.

Jiri Georg Dokoupil has participated in numerous international group exhibitions including the Jinan International Biennale in China (2022), *Art & Publicité* at Centre Pompidou, Paris (1990), the Venice Biennale (1987), Documenta 7 (1982), and *Zeitgeist* at Berlinische Galerie, Martin-Gropius-Bau, Berlin (1982).

He was awarded the Lovis Corinth Prize in 2012 and the Karl Ernst Osthaus-Preis in 2024.

Selected public collections

Neue Galerie – Sammlung Ludwig, Aachen, Germany; FRAC – Picardie, Amiens, France; Caixa de Pensions, Barcelona, Spain; Emanuel Hoffmann-Stiftung, Basel, Switzerland; Hamburger Bahnhof – Museum für Gegenwart, Berlin, Germany; Kupferstichkabinett, Berlin, Germany; Nationalgalerie, Berlin, Germany; Museum Ludwig, Cologne, Germany; Museum Ostwall, Dortmund, Germany; Van Abbemuseum, Eindhoven, The Netherlands; Sammlung Metzger – Museum Folkwang, Essen, Germany; Deutsche Bank. Frankfurt, Germany; Groninger Museum, Groningen, The Netherlands; Horsens Kunstmuseum, Horsens, Denmark; ZKM – Zentrum für Kunst und Medien, Karlsruhe, Germany; CAAM – Centro Atlántico de Arte Moderno, Las Palmas de Gran Canaria. Spain; Hammer Museum, Los Angeles, USA; Museo Nacional Centro de Arte Reina Sofía, Madrid, Spain; CAC – Centro de Arte Contemporáneo de Málaga, Málaga, Spain; Sammlung Pohl, Marburg, Germany; Schaulager, Münchenstein/Basel, Switzerland; Städtische Galerie im Lenbachhaus, Munich, Germany; Sonnabend Collection, New York, USA; Centre Pompidou, Paris, France; Boijmans Van Beuningen, Rotterdam, The Netherlands; National Museum of Contemporary Art, Seoul, Korea; Staatsgalerie, Stuttgart, Germany; Trevi Flash Art Museum of Contemporary Art, Trevi, Italy; Patio Herreriano – Museo de Arte Contemporáneo Español, Valladolid, Spain; Museo de Bellas Artes de Álava, Vitoria-Gasteiz, Spain; Kunstsammlungen zu Weimar – Neues Museum, Weimar, Germany; Städtische Galerie Wolfsburg, Wolfsburg, Germany; Kunsthaus Zürich, Zürich, Switzerland.

REINER OPOKU

Born 1961 in Cologne, Germany.
Curator, manager and art consultant. Living and working in Berlin, Reiner Opoku has curated numerous international art exhibitions since the early 1980s, and is representing a variety of renowned contemporary artists. He also serves as an advisor and initiator for aligning artists and the creative world with institutions, galleries and brands by creating collaboration platforms, publications and commissioned works.

CHRISTIAN DOMÍNGUEZ

Born 1965 in Berlin, Germany. He is an accomplished visual art professional with broad experience in curating and producing exhibitions in different regions of the world as well as an essay writer, poet, editor, film and performance script writer, researcher and amateur anthropologist. One of the main key figures in his life has been the independent curator Harald Szeemann with whom he closely collaborated for many years.

WE ALL COME
FROM AND GO
INTO A BUBBLE.

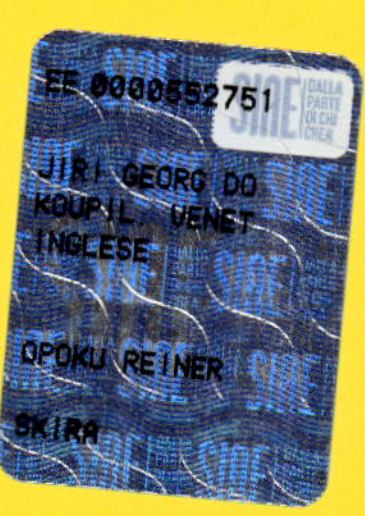

EE 0000552751
SIAE DALLA PARTE DI CHI CREA
JIRI GEORG DO
KOUPIL VENET
INGLESE
OPOKU REINER
SKIRA